Other AUP titles

LEO B HENDRY
Growing Up and Going Out: adolescents and leisure

ALASDAIR ROBERTS
Out to Play: the middle years of childhood

ELLICE MILROY
Role-play: a practical guide

LESLEY GOW and ANDREW McPHERSON
Tell Them From Me: the voices of pupils and school leavers

JOHN BOWLBY *et al*
Rediscovery of the Family and other lectures

NOT FOR SALE

YOUNG PEOPLE IN SOCIETY

Benny Henriksson

translated by
Susan Davies and Irene Scobbie
from the Swedish
Pengarna eller livet

Foreword by Thomas R Forstenzer
Preface by Brian J Ashley

ABERDEEN UNIVERSITY PRESS

First published in English 1983
Aberdeen University Press
A member of the Pergamon Group
Text © Benny Henriksson 1983
Illustrations © Lotta Silfverhjelm 1983

British Library Cataloguing in Publication Data
Henriksson, Benny
   Not for sale
   1. Children—Sweden—History
   I. Title   II. Pengarna eller livet. *English*
   305.2′3′09485   HQ769

   ISBN 0-08-028484-1

PRINTED IN GREAT BRITAIN
THE UNIVERSITY PRESS
ABERDEEN

Foreword

by Thomas R Forstenzer

The publication in English of Benny Henriksson's *Not For Sale* is an early—and fortuitous—sign that International Youth Year (scheduled by the United Nations for 1985) will be marked by considerably more than a few stamp issues and some attractive posters. Like UNESCO's book, *Youth in the 1980s* in which Henriksson's article and some others (including my own) seem to compete for Cassandra honours, *Not For Sale* shows, in its own striking way that, in many regions of the world, to be young is to be at risk: unemployed, underemployed, marginalised, ignored.

Indeed, the themes of International Youth Year—Development, Peace Participation—provide a scorecard of apparent failure and paralysis which few would have predicted ten years ago. Worldwide economic crisis has struck ferociously at the poorest—and most numerous—youth population of the planet: the young of the Third World. The collapse of commodity prices and inflated levels of national debt have stalled development plans in many Third World countries and stranded literally tens of millions of young people who left rural areas for the 'modernising' promise of the cities. They have ended up far from downtown and outside the formal economy in the shantytown, bidonville or barrio. The phenomenon of the village abandoned by all but the aged and infirm means that fields will lie fallow and food production will decline just as urban population soars.

Young people the world over, regardless of the wealth and welfare of their societies, face a threat of war perhaps more intense than at any time since 1945. In the industrialised North of the planet, most young people know—and try to forget—that they live on ground zero and that billions are spent to make the unthinkable more plausible every day. And conventional wars (supersonic, computerised but as yet, non-nuclear) have broken out at an accelerating pace both north and south of the Equator, leaving borders and issues still unresolved but soldiers and civilians quite irreversibly dead and maimed.

Finally, the young who suffer the results of the world's failure to promote development and assure peace are rarely asked to participate in the local, national, and international decisions which will shape their adult lives and those of their children. (We too often forget that it is during 'youth' that men and women begin families.)

The dubious honour of being considered a working model of a possible future is given to few places and countries. Sweden is one of them. Yet, for Henriksson, Sweden is a model which should warn more than beckon. Drawing on the American historian, Christopher Lasch, and his controversial and troubling vision of the emptiness of modern life in the richest and most well-organised societies, Henriksson shows that Swedish youth has found no 'Haven in a Heartless World'. Going beyond Lasch, he proposes an alternative organisation of everyday life which will challenge every sectarian at every point on the political spectrum.

At the same time sweepingly radical and deeply conservative, the argument and programme of *Not For Sale* rejects aseptic, quantified, expert-dominated and institutionalized 'welfare' concepts. The centripetal pull of the benevolent, humanitarian welfare state creates a vacuum of privatization and irresponsibility around individuals and a void of passivity and drift within the young themselves. The welfare world is so slick and shiny that young people are prevented from getting a grip on authentic experiences and feelings: work, responsibility, love, and caring. It is so rationally organised that the young are set apart from adults, the aged, the sick and the dying. 'Who am I?', perhaps *the* definitional question of adolescence is answered by the anguish of 'waiting': waiting for a job, waiting for work which is satisfying, waiting to be fully grown up and waiting to be a full, responsible participant in life's decisions.

Not For Sale would be a poor choice for bed-time reading by anyone who expects the young to be uncritically thankful for the struggles and achievements of the past. It clearly demonstrates that International Youth Year must begin with the injunction: listen and learn about your world from those whose eyes are newer.

Dr Thomas Forstenzer, a social historian and a consultant to UNESCO, is on the staff of the United Nations Centre for Social Development and Humanitarian Affairs, Vienna.

Contents

Preface

by Brian J Ashley

This preface, for the English speaking reader and particularly the British public, must demonstrate the relevance and importance of a Swedish book to that wider readership. There is no doubt about the importance and relevance of the subject to all advanced Western societies.

This book is concerned to highlight the social and economic situation of young people. It presents a very clear picture of the critical position of youth in the grip of a modern commercial system which holds the consumer as a helpless prisoner within its trends and fashions. The search for profit dictates the policy decisions of that system, and the welfare and development of a generation of youth is, in the opinion of the author, being surrendered to the satisfaction of material needs which are themselves created by the system which supplies the readymade answers.

This picture, based upon a careful and extensive inquiry among Swedish youth, is not, of course, new and is familiar to most advanced societies. Some twenty years ago Mark Abrams pointed to the same phenomenon in Britain through his book, *The Teenage Consumer.*

That, however, is in itself significant because certainly the problem still exists without amelioration within British society. British youth workers, at present, await the results of a government revue of the youth service in the hope that a new formula may be found. The Manpower Services Commission in Britain continually launches new programmes, with questionable results. The United Kingdom Commission for Racial Equality, of which I am a member, has identified young people as a primary target for its programme for the elimination of racial discrimination and the promotion of equal opportunity. In Scotland I recently chaired an official working party inquiring into the affairs of youth: our report emphasised the national concern for the position of young people and the doubts about a solution built upon the methods and organisations which at present exist in modern societies. In British social work circles the recent Barclay report emphasises the need to find new approaches to the concept of care in the community.

This book which attempts to present just such a new answer to both the situation of youth and the concept of care deserves to be read carefully at this time. All advanced societies, based upon a competitive commercial system, are faced with the problems of maintaining that system under the pressure of a world depression. Among the widespread consequences is the effect upon a younger generation who are bearing the brunt of that depression due to the lack of employment possibilities. In a society based upon productive work and competitive endeavour it is difficult for young people without work to feel a sense of value and worth or to see a future of personal development. The problem is compounded by the fact that the resources necessary to give public expression to a caring concern for their situation are being drastically reduced by the same failure of the economic system.

This Swedish book challenges the assumption that a solution must be found which assumes the perpetuation of that same system. In presenting an alternative solution, the author presents an argument based on a clear sense of commitment to a cooperative caring community and upon an ideological position which questions the need to pursue increasing productivity towards greater materialism and which substitutes the conception of rendering equal value to the caring and concerned activities of the community.

Whilst many readers will not be able to enter fully into that degree of commitment nor, necessarily, able to comprehend the reversal of the current materialistic objectives of our societies, nevertheless the carefully argued solution which is presented is challenging and must be worthy of consideration.

Indeed it is incumbent upon all readers who are concerned about the situation of present day young people and their future to try to find an acceptable alternative if we reject the solution proposed in this book. Certainly the *ad hoc* and piecemeal approaches to the principle of community care within most welfare societies have met with only limited success, if not dismal failure.

Often by examining the work of anthropologists who describe other societies we may come to a better understanding of our own society. Also the careful examination of someone else's situation can often throw new light upon our own situation. The English speaking reader should be reminded that Sweden, in the space of the past two generations, has moved from a rural society, through industrialisation, to one of the most advanced and affluent societies in Western Europe. During the latter half of that period Sweden has devoted a greater proportion of her economic wealth than most societies towards creating a more advanced system of social welfare. Therefore, this examination of that process of Swedish industrialisation and the resulting situation for Swedish youth, together with a total reexamination of the system of caring within that society, can be used as a mirror within which other societies can see their own problems and even their own future a little more clearly.

Mr Brian J. Ashley is Director of the School of Community Studies, Moray House College of Education, Edinburgh, Scotland

Introduction

When the Swedish National Youth Council published *Ej till salu* (*Not for Sale*), Sweden's largest ever youth report, in June 1981, we were of course very keen to see the reactions. In all, nine reports were published during the three years the investigation on commercial youth culture was underway. *Ej till salu* is the final report of the study. Was this with its 650 pages to become yet another national 'tome' to be put on the bookshelf . . . ? We had already stuck our necks out many times and been the subject of criticism and debate. For example, when we tried, in one of the reports, to discuss the content and message of commerical films and the advertising methods of the large film companies, we were accused of only wishing to introduce bans and censorship. That's often the climate of debate in the Swedish mass-media.

So, when we took on the task, in *Ej till salu*, of not only criticising the market for its cynical exploitation of children and adolescents, but also of bringing out the negative effects on children and adolescents of changes in society, we risked challenging even more people. In *Not for Sale* we try to understand *why* commercialised leisure and cultural activities constitute such an important part of our lives, both as adults and children. In order to understand 'the commercial magnet' it is not enough just to criticise advertising methods. Understanding also has to be on a different level. We had to delve quite deeply into Swedish social history to find the clues. We discovered that Swedish society, like most Western societies, had not only undergone a tremendous social and material development; this development had also fundamentally changed the situation of children. Parallel to the growth of the market we saw how the state intervened. The Welfare State, which is so characteristic of 'the Swedish model', certainly provides social service—but what happens to people's chances of participation and to common responsibility for social care? Among other things, the book deals with the way professionally trained experts declare parents incapable of bringing up their children, and undervalue old-fashioned everyday competence. This makes parents and other adults unsure and afraid of bringing up their children and influencing them ideologically. The responsibility is taken over by the institutions. The children of the local community become the children of the State.

What then are the collective effects of social changes on children's lives? Children and adolescents have no productive functions in the modern Welfare State, instead they live in a period of waiting, a vacuum of leisure and consumption, which produces a lack of self-confidence and a negative belief in the future. Children have become separated more and more from the 'ordinary' adult. Children especially miss the company of men, who are more or less invisible in children's lives. What does this have to do with commercialism? Well, the market provides children with a new role instead of the one denied them. The role of consumer has become more and more important, while young people have lost their functions and adults have become distanced from them. The market sells identification with idols, it provides children with experiences, knowledge, companionship, fantasy and myths. But it costs money and the objects of identification are constantly being replaced by new ones. Children live in a state of permanent temporariness.

At the same time, Swedish children long for better contact with adults. The experiences of television and video are no substitute for direct contact with adults. In all their lists of what they would like to have in the future, social contact with adults always comes before possessions. Most children and adolescents are satisfied with the material standard they have. *Materially satiated but socially starved.*

Was this the price we had to pay for economic expansion, development and success? Is this a hint of the hangover of the welfare state?

This analysis ought already to have angered all of those who believe in positive legislated social development as a set result of economic growth and Western ideals of progress. But our proposals for solutions were also threatened with being dismissed as unrealistic and naive. We maintain that it is possible to change and develop our society in a way which will also make children participants in the life of the community. We present an optimistic programme.

However, the realisation of this demands other social changes than those which we have been familiar with. Perhaps we can describe them as a 'counterpoint' in the 'current' of the political deliberations we have been used to until now.

We aim the searchlight at a forgotten sector in society which belongs neither to the Market nor to the State. It is a free, informal, economic sector where children and adolescents have productive functions alongside adults. The base for this 'caring economy' is everyday life in the local communities.

We outline a programme for building up, or saving and re-creating this sector, which is of course also the environment in which children grow up. It will become the base for creating better conditions for child development, for opposing the Market, for finding new ways of organising social care and for developing co-operative models of ownership. To carry out work within the caring economy will become a right *and* an obligation both for children, adolescents, adults and the elderly. Everyone has a part to play.

Challenging the whole of Sweden's welfare model and presenting totally new models for development—can we be taken seriously? These proposals surely would be sufficient grounds for a government investigation to be totally silenced. But this has not happened. On the contary, the report has stimulated great debate. The little Youth Council, one of Sweden's smallest government bureaux, was almost overwhelmed with demands for collaboration in courses, at conferences, on college courses, in local authorities and schools. At the time of writing, October 1982, *Ej till salu* (the lengthy report), has been introduced to approximately 30,000 people at conferences alone. Approximately 15,000 copies of the 650-page *Ej till salu* have been sold in Sweden. Approximately 15,000 copies of the summary, *Pengarna eller livet,* which has here been translated into English, with the title *Not for Sale,* have also been sold and used as material for debate and study. The result of this may be seen in the bulky files where we have collected all communications and letters which have been sent to the Youth Council from associations and organisations with political, trades union, religious and other identities; from public authorities at all levels; from schools and other educational institutions. The pedagogical idea behind this method of working has been to stimulate a 'process of reconsideration', where many people participate, not just centrally located politicians and bureaucrats.

What are the reactions then? Most people agree with the description we have given of the changed conditions of adolescents. Our picture of the marginalisation and vulnerability of adolescents is confirmed especially by those who work directly with young people—teachers, club leaders, school psychologists etc.

The proposals are also taken seriously by most people. There is hardly anyone who does not want the future society which we have outlined. But there is, of course, also criticism. There are those who do not believe that any social changes can be achieved without our first changing the economic system of our country. We may call them the red critics. But there are also those who believe that our proposals threaten entirely the free market economy and would mean revolution. We may call them the blue critics. A surprisingly large number of people are, however, behind the idea that we need a completely new perspective and that the present models for development are just not enough. We may perhaps call this direction red-green, since it often points out that solutions must be found within another dimension than the traditional right/left scale.

A number of people criticise us for not giving any clues as to how we shall be able to realise our proposals. This criticism is both correct and incorrect. It is easier to paint a picture of a future society than it is to show in a tangible form the way in which we may reach this state. Many people have pointed out that there are many strong forces which oppose the development which we propose. Are the obstacles too great? But would it not be wrong for a government enquiry to lay out all courses of action for the movement which must grow out of the popular movements and local needs? A movement towards new solutions which is already underway not only in Sweden but also in many places in the industrialised world. More and more people are searching for new lifestyles and solutions for social life. It is like a massive conspiracy from grassroots level against the established situation. What the politicians and the local and state authorities have to do is to decide on whether support is to be given to people's own responsibilities or whether obstacles are to be put in the way. By my understanding, the choice is clear. Judging by the many letters we have received from local authorities which wish to be part of development work for the creation of functioning local environments, they are also thinking along the same lines.

It is worth mentioning yet another reaction. I often get different reactions from men and women. The women often say that the proposals are good—they safeguard the things for which women have always had responsibility. But men often argue that the proposals are divorced from reality. It is thought, for example, that our proposals on lowering working hours in industry, in order to gain more time for constructing a functioning, caring economy, are unrealistic now when we have to 'get ourselves out of the economic crisis through production'. The reactions are naturally linked to the traditional sex roles and division of labour for men and women. Men have never shown any especially great interest in getting involved in social care. Women have always borne the burden of child upbringing, tending and caring, as unpaid work in the home or as paid employment in the public sector. It is the man who has dominated political life and association activities, while women have often had the direct experience of contact with children and adolescents, the infirm and the old. Women see more clearly the crises of social environments. However, it would be very serious if men, in the future too, chose not to involve themselves in local caring work. On the contrary, it would be extremely valuable if they did so. It would be important for children's development, and it would give men new experiences of inestimable value.

In the report we discuss caring work as both a right and an obligation. Most people react negatively to the introduction of some kind of civil community service by means of legislation. That opinion is understandable. But against the background of the different reactions of men and women, we often put forward, somewhat lightheartedly, the idea that caring work should perhaps be voluntary for women and obligatory for men.

We hope that *Not for Sale* will also stimulate debate in other countries. We know, through our international contacts, that there is a great deal of interest in discussing the contents of the report in other countries, too.

It has seemed natural and important to try and test the Swedish debate in the international community. The Youth Council sees this English edition as a concrete contribution to the exchange of ideas before the International Year of Youth in 1985, which has the theme 'Peace, participation, development'. This may give us an opportunity of discussing in earnest the conditions for growing up which we offer our children and adolescents. We hope that this book will be able to contribute to such a discussion.

Our next task is to carry out an international study with the aim of studying various preconditions for the participation of children and adolescents in Sweden and in other countries in both the Northern and the Southern hemispheres.

As one component in this work we place great importance on widening and deepening our international contacts by way of spontaneous comments stimulated by this book. Such contact may be made directly with the National Youth Council, Krukmakargatan 19, 116 51 Stockholm.

This is also the place to extend a very warm thanks for the fine translation of *Not for Sale* which was done by Susan Davies and Irene Scobbie of the Department of Scandinavian Studies at the University of Aberdeen, and also to Colin MacLean, of AUP, who quite daringly thought it worthwhile to publish a Swedish youth study in English.

Benny Henriksson
Stockholm, October 1982

1   Children in the rural community

In the first four chapters, we describe the changing role of children in society, seen in historical perspective. In the first chapter this description will deal mainly with 'children of the rural community', that is, with the conditions for those growing up in the pre-industrial society and how social changes during the decades immediately before and after the turn of the century have affected the child's situation. Throughout history we can see how children have been exploited. We can also see the clear division between the children of the gentry and of the peasantry. We report on how the attitudes towards children and childhood have changed, first in the higher strata of society, so that new ideals for the upbringing and care of children were developed.

Children in farm production

Concepts such as family, childhood, adolescence, are, historically speaking, relatively new. In pre-industrial society, the basic social cell was the 'household'; the farm and daily life among people who lived under the same roof. This comprised the family as we see it today, but the household also included other adults, relatives, grandmothers, grandfathers, maids and farmhands. The farm combined community life and cultural life within the rural areas. What we would call the nuclear family, that is, man and wife plus their children, fitted into this household and also into a larger social pattern. They lived a localised but nevertheless public life. The word 'family' came into use much later.[1]

[1] Notes are on pp. 195, 6.

The way parents brought up their children was practical and concrete. As soon as the child was free from its mother's apron strings, it was expected to make itself useful. The child participated in the adult world at an early age and became, in a sense, a complement to the adults. There were inumerable opportunities to learn both everyday tasks and the more demanding skills by participating in the daily round. Thus, everyday customs were passed on by many adults and old people, with whom all the children had some personal relationship. Upbringing was an inter-generational process, between those who knew and those who did not.[2] Culture in the form of knowledge, norms and morals was conveyed and developed from generation to generation. Adults were more or less united in wanting to preserve the prevailing view of the world. It was important to preserve the experiences and wisdom of life which others had acquired. Learning now from the past was the best preparation for the future. Grandparents could not envisage any other kind of future for their grandchildren than their own past. Thus every individual lived the life of both his ancestors and descendants and the generations were bound together. The past also bore the future, even if this future was an adaptation of the old.

The old folk on the farm had an important role to play. They represented memories, myths, songs, patterns of life, fear of the Day of Judgement, wood nymphs and spirits.[3] Myths afforded both fear and comfort. If one kept on the right side of 'the little people', they would help protect people and animals against evil spirits and ill-fortune. Life was greatly dependent upon the local resources of the community. Time was not short in the modern sense. Daily existence could easily become monotonous. Rootlessness, loneliness and alienation were outside people's normal experiences.[4]

Work was strictly divided with clear boundaries between man's work and woman's work. Men and women alike were responsible for what we would call the *production,* i.e. producing the necessities of life, equipment etc. In addition, the women had charge of the *social reproduction*, i.e. all the work involved in recreating and renewing the pattern of everyday life and passing on the social heritage from one generation to another: children, invalids and old people were used as the channels. Women have been able to assert themselves more in communities where they were able to combine their reproductive role with important functions, rather than in communities where such a combination was more difficult.[5] The children had to learn, early in life, their sex role in work and in social life, but even if work was guided by sexual differentiation, man and wife very often worked side by side. For the children it often afforded countless opportunities to benefit from their parents' skills and to understand their authority.

Production and reproduction were also guided by another important social institution connected with division of labour—the *patriarchy* or male dominance. In this way, the man was master of household production and of its servants, while as the father he was in charge of domestic order. The fathers' authority watched over behaviour, discipline and sexual morals, and thus the interests of the family and its heritage.[6]

The law considered woman weaker and inferior to man, unintelligent and dependent upon a man's protection. Even if woman was subordinate to man in all respects, she was, however, still esteemed and important in the farming economy. A Swedish farmer's wife was responsible for a large proportion of the domestic economy. A farm could not run without its mistress.

Our view of childhood as a time free from work, a time for play and schooling is also, historically speaking, quite a new phenomenon.[7] The child entered adult society at an early age and carried out useful tasks. Adolescents participated in production or were apprenticed at some other farm or to some other master. Slowly but surely they were trained in the demands of adult life by taking on new tasks progressively. Different initiation rites marked the transition, stage by stage, from childhood to adulthood. Authority in its different forms laid down the limits to freedom. Customs varied from region to region. When a young man joined the local group of youths, he was not only mature enough to work but also to organise festivities or nightly courting visits.[8]

The rural community set its limits

The rural community was in control of its children. The social units were easy to relate to and public in a different way to today's large

3

society. Social control must have felt constricting, with many adults keeping an eye on the children at the same time. It was dependent on people's total reliance on others who were in the same vulnerable position as themselves, or who were even worse off. Local social control was built into daily life. The upbringing of children takes place within a network of social relationships in which parents, among others, were included; they were not alone however, but were guided in many ways by the public moral code of the community.[9]

We must not for a moment overlook the beating, ill-treatment and humiliation which were a feature of our forefathers' childhoods. Infant mortality due to disease, poverty, neglect or accidents was common. People were kept strictly to their station. A large proportion of the rural population were poor crofters, cotters, farmhands and servants. Even further down the scale were vagabonds and tramps.[10] 'The history of childhood is a nightmare from which we have only recently begun to awaken,' says Lloyd de Mause,[11] the historian. Social control with its two faces of constraint and support, of limitations and guidelines, of intrusion and sociability has, in many ways, been lost in the transition from poor farming society to modern industrial nation. It is only natural for us to draw attention to this in an historical survey.

Two kinds of children

Throughout the history of childhood we can see the division between the children of the gentry and of the peasantry. In the pre-industrial society the differences were obvious, as in the early period of industrialisation. Working-class children grew up with the other children in the district, on the streets and in backyards. Only for a favoured few did the years of childhood mean a sheltered environment with a nursemaid and a well-appointed nursery. The class distinctions still persist. In most studies of childhood and adolescence, there exist today the same differences between children from different environments. Today's problems affect children in different ways. This book, therefore, will concentrate on describing the situation of those who fare worst or live in the worst environments. This does not mean that the problems and menacing images which we touch upon do not affect all children, but that certain groups, even today, are more adversely affected than others.

Middle-class children

We shall first see how the view of children is influenced by the development of society and the break away from the old village and peasant society around the end of the nineteenth century.

A new view of the family and childhood gradually gained a foothold in the higher echelons of the early industrial society. When old patriarchal principles for transferring power and wealth crumbled, new methods of showing one's position in society were required. Upbringing, education and culture would now draw up the boundaries between the new middle classes and the peasants and workers. The new middle classes also wanted to establish that *their* children were different from the 'ignorant' children of the proletariat. This was done by 'inaugurating' childhood. The child was seen as both imperfect, in need of a long and strict training, and yet innocent and pure, in need of care and attention. Children were no longer considered incomplete adults but small personalities in their own right and with their own weaknesses. Children in the higher social classes were 'liberated' from work and their lives were filled instead with play, games and school. Adults wanted to invest in their children's future.[12]

At the same time the conception of the home and family was changing. The emotional bonds within the family were emphasised rather than the productional ones. Love was the cement to bind man and wife together. Parental love was the guiding star in relations between the generations. Intimacy and closeness were sought within the small family, which gradually became the obvious centre of married life. The family was separated from

kindred and farm household. Here the distinction between a *public* and *private* sphere was being formed.

The new middle-class families almost made the home and their own nuclear family into a cult. The family provided a shelter from the outside world, an opportunity for the men to flee from the unfeeling world of work to the emotional, loving communion of the family. The family became the vehicle for allowing the middle classes to show off their new capacity for consumption. Growing affluence provided scope for the middle classes to invest in larger houses and fine furniture. Here one could retreat from the company of others. The history of the bedroom and nursery illustrates the way family relations have become private and intimate.[13]

Affording leisure

It was also the new middle classes who could afford to emphasise the difference between *work* and *leisure*. The modern concept of leisure was brought into being here. In the middle-class world, people could afford leisure for the first time. They even began to have problems in filling in their leisure time.[14]

Expenditure on leisure is an outward sign of the consumer's status, demonstrating the group he belongs to and his desired identity. In anonymous surroundings the reasons for being seen and noticed increases. It is the same phenomenon—the search for identity and recognition—which today's commercial teenage market so skilfully exploits. Travel and excursions. The old fishing coastline becomes a leisure coast for the middle classes. People drive out to the country for rest and relaxation, and live in the country in the summer. We get the first leisure organisations, charities for the ladies and societies and clubs for the gentlemen, not to be confused with the popular movements which at almost the same time began to be established amongst the working-class and peasant movements. But while the middle classes arranged festivities and discussed hobbies, the workers and peasants slept in order to cope with the next day's hard work.[15] Leisure was not yet established among them at the end of the nineteenth century.

Refinement and education

The new middle-class view of the world affects our whole conception of culture. Culture becomes refined culture; workers' and peasants' culture is not culture but non-culture. Culture becomes synonymous with education, refinement and discipline. In fact it is culture which has divided the middle classes from the uncivilised peasantry or from the crude masses of workers who were not considered to have any education or culture at all. Emotions, experiences, folk dances and music are not culture. Emotional experiences and culture are classified as leisure and are ritualised in refined dancing and theatre productions.[16]

The middle classes want to prepare their children for future responsibilities in society. Upbringing and study become an important part of the preparations, especially for boys. In earlier times, children in rural society had inherited their position. Now the new middle stratum had to win their positions by way of education, so that the family property would be guaranteed. Educational ideals became in this way the cornerstone of a liberal revolution. These ideals were combined with a desire to quell social unrest and to control the children of the growing working classes and were gradually united in the demand for public elementary schooling. In addition the technical advances of industry were making children uneconomic.[17] Instead of participating in production, children were to be kept and educated in preparation for their *future* role in working life.

At the same time, however, school was to preserve the social stratification which was so important to the middle classes. Admittedly the elementary school did provide both high and low with the same skills, but the skills were those of the higher orders, and the school would soon single out the children of the upper classes. They

9

would go on to grammar schools and higher education, while the working-class and peasant children would have to make do with the education they received at elementary school. It was not least the expense and the loss of contribution to the family budget which prevented children from poor homes being able to continue their education.

Working-class children at work and at school

While the middle classes were building their new image of the family and childhood, the childhood years of working-class children were filled with hard work. With the rise of industrialism more and more people left agriculture for other work. Increasing numbers were attracted to the factories. Cheap labour was in great demand. It was therefore common in the tobacco, match and glass industries to employ children aged between 7 and 13. They did not start work to learn a trade but were employed because they were so cheap and so that they could contribute to the family budget. Child labour cost only a third of adult male labour. But the children's work was often as hard and strenuous as that of their elders. Sometimes they had to perform work which adults could not manage, such as creeping along narrow mineshafts. They had to work from morning to late at night. Their existence was far removed from the Carl Larsson idyll of childhood.

For the working classes, the struggle during this critical period was about a more tolerable existence, to escape from their poverty, to get better housing, to tackle childhood diseases, to let their own children have a share in the 'good' education. These were the aims for the working classes. Many middle-class advantages became working-class goals. At the same time, there was a deep class identity which preserved family ties, neighbourly co-operation and the more open family. Workers at the turn of the century were the sons and daughters of the rural proletariat. They brought with them social patterns, close contacts with the local public, family and friends and thus also resistance to middle-class family culture.

Within the labour movement there were also strong demands for education for all. Many working-class parents saw schooling as a means of breaking the degrading class ties and poverty and of giving their children the education and occupations which they themselves had never been able to have.[19] There were therefore many different forces which were united in the demand for compulsory schooling, but it was middle-class ideology which provided the contents for school tuition.

Then the young people played together, split up into teams—played football and rounders. They didn't start to think about boys and things until they were older. They could live out more of their childhood. Now everybody gets grown up so awfully quickly. Perhaps not grown up, but concerned about their appearance, self-centred. A lot of them get into gangs as early as 11–12 years old. OK, I usually go sledging with my neighbour who is a few years younger than me, although most people laugh at me. But when my grandmother was young large crowds would meet and go sledging down long slopes. At least I think it was like that.

Pia, aged 14

People on the move

The old peasant society was swiftly being transformed into an industrial state. Society was undergoing great change. Industrialisation, population growth, immigration and emigration. The children of rural society became the children of the middle-class and industrial workers.

Social problems, alcohol abuse and above all poverty caused social unrest. On occasion the situation approached open revolt and the authorities felt threatened. They wanted, therefore, to see the new middle classes' living patterns and attitude to home, family, childhood, youth, education and culture spread to the workers and peasants. But their ambitions were two-fold. It would,

11

of course, be a good thing for the lower orders to devote themselves to middle-class attitudes, but the classes must nevertheless keep themselves to themselves. It was not a question, therefore, of sacrificing one's privileges or of working for equality. The aim was simply to let middle-class morality subdue social unrest.

Meanwhile, the workers, for their part, had started to get organised, to unite to deal with their everyday hardships and to form associations. Liberal associations were actually their models, but their ideology and demands were obviously different. Craft associations were formed first, and then, towards the middle of the nineteenth century, trades unions. The first genuine popular movements were formed in the second half of the nineteenth century, that melting pot of old and new,[20] by social reshuffling, by the desire for changes and improvements but also in the knowledge that it was essential to rescue and preserve cultural patterns and identity. The popular movements struggled for better working conditions and reasonable wages, but also for education and for what we today would call general community activities and entertainment. In this way, two conflicting views of the future developed, one characterised by the conception of leisure as pleasure, relaxation, hobbies and pastimes, the other rather more by voluntary community work and an ideological struggle but where struggle and community were fused into one.[21]

Working class environments had identical conditions and living patterns. People shared common hardships and the same clearly defined enemies. Thus the struggle and community spirit united the workers and formed the basis for what we call class identity, that is to say, they did not only share the same convictions, the same political political values, but also the same experiences of life which led to those convictions. Wherever the labour movement was organised, the vast majority of its members belonged to the working classes. The environments were demarcated and there was a neighbourhood feeling. Places of work were close to housing areas. Almost everyone living in the same district worked at the same place. Overcrowding and social problems were not and could not be considered individual problems. Neighbours and acquaintances were wrestling with the same problems as oneself; it was natural, therefore, to turn towards movements with suggested collective solutions and improvements. In this way working-class environments constituted communities and sub-cultures within the predominant social culture.

For decades the popular movements organised the Swedish people, in the face of strong opposition from those who held power in society. The aims and dreams of a better society drove them on. The Free Church movement, the temperance movement, the labour movement, the agrarian movement, the co-operative movement, the athletics movement—they all built up a democratic tradition which is unique. In no other country have popular movements had so much significance as in Sweden.

But the old popular movements were also dominated by the remnants of the patriarchal system, which the men brought with them and which led to male dominance in the movements. Among other things, this meant that the popular movements, too, concentrated their political demands on those areas dominated by men's conditions, i.e. production, paid work and public life. Things closer to home, care of children, the sick and old and the unpaid work traditionally carried out by women, were excluded from what was defined as politically important. In many cases special women's organisations were formed outside or within the traditional popular movements, to guard women's rights. Even if questions of equality were discussed at an early stage, however, the position of women and their infleunce in society and in the popular movements were not taken up seriously until much later.

Children on the move

Child and youth organisations were gradually separated from the traditional popular movements.[23] Here the wish to have children trained in the work and responsibilities of the democratic process coincided with the view of childhood and youth as special phases in life. In a sense, the popular movements which excluded children, encouraged a division between the adult world and the world of childhood. The general trend in society towards specialisaton and sectorisation accelerated the creation of children's organisations.

But there were other reasons, too. A desire on the part of parents within the popular movements to educate and influence their children ideologically. Criticism of the religious training given in schools led both the free churches and the labour movement to start their own Sunday schools. Even if expectations were too optimistic and the time not yet ripe, this does reflect a conviction that it was essential to convey one's values to the coming generation. Working-class parents realised that their children would not automatically become politically aware, or that they would not become so through the school's teaching, which tended on the contrary to oppose this. But there was a great deal of criticism from society. The socialistic Sunday schools were called 'scoffers' schools'. Many working class parents also seemed doubtful.[24] The state church and the middle class school had a monopoly on ideological education. They did not wish to release it to their challengers.

In 1910, there were already 2200 Christian youth organisations with 113,000 members. Out of the labour movement's Sunday schools grew the socialistic children's clubs, whose members were aged from 12 to 16. What the adults had started the young people carried on themselves. Gradually the first youth club was founded. With enormous success, the labour movement introduced, at the beginning of the twentieth century, the so-called 'story times'. Children streamed into the Community Halls. There they learned about their class origins, about fighting for a more just society; they were to be trained to work for the labour movement. The children learned a very different moral code from that taught in schools. Instead of obedience and gratitude, the 'story time' movement told them, in its own Ten Commandments, that they should stand up for their rights and defend themselves against oppression.[25]

But movements professing other values also became popular. Baden-Powell's Boy Scouts, for instance, were taught to be 'men in the true sense of the word'. Courage, endurance, strength, thrift, honesty, decency and self-discipline were among the movement's guiding ideals. The boys were to be sharpened up to manhood. Thus the ideologists clashed over the aims of education, but common to both was a clear awareness of the importance of ideological influence and education.[26]

2 The State assumes responsibility

In this chapter we shall move on from early industrialism to the present day. We shall see how the state or official bodies intervene more and more to counteract difficulties arising from such things as industrialism and the market economy. This also means that the state intervenes increasingly in family life, first through charity, then via doctors and science, and finally assuming ultimate responsibility for the care and upbringing of children. While a strong welfare state has been being built up, we have also become an extremely professionalised society where people's common concerns have been taken over by the state. We shall be critically examining the effects of this.

If we can talk of children of the rural society, in the pre-industrial and early industrial period, we shall see in this chapter how responsibility for the child has been taken over by the public institutions, or the *state* in the broad sense of the term, so that, by the mid-twentieth century, we can talk of the *child of the state*. The development of society from early industrialism onwards gave us contradictory messages, and for the family and children it appeared to be pulling in different directions. Households became private homes whilst the state took over more and more of the parents' responsibility for their children.

Charity comes cheap

Charity organisations, the philanthropists, were responsible for the first real socio-political developments in Sweden, as in so many other European countries.[1] Through state support they became an important link in the state's increasing interest in the family and the child. With their own particular moral code they saw problems as either 'neglect' or 'depravity', that is, according to them society must intervene both against children who were 'living dangerously' and those who were 'dangerous'.

There was social unrest in the country at the outset of industrialism. The emergent labour movement demanded tangible improvements. The situation occasionally came close to open revolt. The authorities considered that too much poverty caused too much discontent. Social liberalism demanded reforms, therefore, while wishing to control and preserve the social order. Another factor was a kind of social economy which aimed at minimising public costs in order to deal with poverty and secure a sufficiently large work force. Charity was a welcome response to all these demands.[2] The *philanthropists* not only gave expression to a humane view of mankind which would save those who were worst off, but also passed on middle-class patterns of home and family as an ideal of the restless working classes. In this way order would be maintained. This moralising philanthropy set the working-class woman's domain inside the home. Women should be prepared for family life by domestic training. Competition between men and women could be stopped by giving status to a woman's domestic work. There was a campaign for homes large enough to be hygenic but small enough to house only the nuclear family. Houses would be so constructed that parents could be intimate without their children observing them, but so that they could nevertheless keep an eye on the children. Attempts were made to segregate the sexes and age-groups in workers' homes, but this ran so counter to folk traditions that it took the philanthropists a century to carry out. What was involved was the transition from a household connected with production, to a home based on seclusion from the outside world, on internal supervision and consumption.[3]

The philanthropic movement gained political power. Its greatest energies were focused on offering moral advice, which was cheaper and would make the poor refrain from bad habits. It encouraged thrift and desired to make poor families independent of community help and free from old dependences and solidarity. The virtues of a secure family life were preached everywhere, in parliamentary debates and the weekly magazines, by Ellen Key, Carl Larsson and Elsa Beskow. This independence involved, among other things, a shift from the public moral code to the private, one of the cornerstones in what we call the privatisation of the family.

Science, hygiene and morality

Medical research made society open its eyes to the living conditions of poor families. Doctors were also equipped with innumerable instructions and advice on how families ought to live. Aided by this hygienic and moral guidance, doctors promoted the middle-class cult of home and family. The family became a part of the disciplining of the force while the old authorities were challenged. A new moral code based on scientific evidence thereby supplanted the old centres of power in society, the myths, the Church, the patriarchy and the wise old women. This did not necessarily mean that the power had been deposed. It assumed other guises. 'The power of the black coats was replaced by the white.'[4] Old tradition and everyday skills were succeeded by science. The doctors allied themselves, above all, with women in the home in challenging patriarchy. The doctors' moral code was to be spread with the aid of women. 'The doctors prescribed and the women carried it out.' Thus the women became the family's moral guardian. They would make the home so pleasant that the husband would not be tempted to go to the pub and the young would not hang about on the streets in the evening. The alliance between doctor, teacher and mother would annihilate the family as 'a pocket of resistance'. Poor women's domestic work would be elevated into a profession. A fund of unpaid work would compensate for social costs, introduce hygiene into childcare and nutritional habits to the working classes and instil regular habits. The members of a working-class family formed a chain of supervision, holding each other in check against the temptations of the outside world. For working-class children this view and the reforms which grew out of it meant a kind of supervised freedom, instead of growing up having to fend for themselves. In this way the doctors' incursion into family life was a further step in the state's steadily growing control of family life. The alliance between mother and doctor made it easier for society to influence and govern the family.

The philanthropists' and doctors' crusading zeal goes hand in hand with new *scientific* interpretations of difficulties encountered by children and families. With the help of medical science and later of psychology and psychiatry, all kinds of perversities and deviations from the 'norm' are introduced among those who are living in a difficult situation or who in some other way deviate from the usual patterns. Science classifies, finds symptoms and makes problems of things which were earlier a part of social life or had their roots in social living conditions. In these scientific interpretations, children's difficulties, their normal aggressions or sexual games become diseases and faults which can only be treated or removed by specially trained experts. Parents grow uncertain about their children's upbringing or what relationship they should have with them. The parents are made allies in the hunt for symptoms and deviations. The 'correct' knowledge about children and experiences of their lives is collected within the new circle of trained professionals. Admittedly the work of the philanthropists and doctors and the new psychological sciences mean that social attitudes became more human and that the old institutions of power are challenged, but at the same time the old power is being replaced by a new one.

The State takes over

Thus the state begins to assume ultimate responsibility for the child. Early intervention is the authorities' and child experts' guiding principle—to do something before it is too late. The state's 'obligation' and 'inescapable duty' to provide care and education and the child's *right* to these 'advantages' are emphasised. The Child Welfare Act of 1926 states that the state may make a decision about the protection and care of the child even against its parents' wishes. This was something quite new. It was a distinct amalgam of humane and social demands for improvements in the child's circumstances with traces of new forms of social control, separations and a rejection of the parents as guardians and protectors.

The philanthropists' demands for control and general education led, among other things, to individual means-tested social legislation. Every request for economic aid was to be examined for moral errors that had caused the problems. In this policy the question of morals was systematically coupled with the family's financial situation, while the family could be kept under observation.[6]

Philanthropy moderated the labour movement's political demands and prepared the ground for a large proportion of the future social policy of the authorities. The charity workers' idealistic work was taken over gradually by the authorities and their new professional groups, social workers, psychologists, etc.

From charity to welfare

An enormous development transformed Sweden from a poor country into one of the materially richest countries in the world. Social misery in the early industrial period was almost incomprehensibly great. Degradation and wretched housing were common problems, especially in the large towns. Demands for social reforms grew stronger. The demands followed two lines: moralising philanthropy and social policy based on group solidarity. The latter emerged from the social politics of the popular movements. Within social policy the division is seen most clearly between individual means-tested social assistance and the demands for social reforms for all.

In the post-war period the labour movement was in government and had the chance to realise many of the social reforms that had been on their programme for so long. Following the Wigforss line, the cost of social policies was no longer considered as an economic burden on society but it was realised that it could also stimulate the economy. Social welfare was created out of the surplus from the post-war 'harvest years'.[7] Industry expanded and there was a large growth in the economy. The problems of the market economy were dealt with by social 'safety nets'. When Swedish society flourished in the post-war period, this was brought about by great efficiency, technical skill and progress, and rationalisation. The economic boom led to low unemployment and the Swedes achieved a material standard of living without equal in the world. A series of socio-political reforms could be introduced for the most needy. Welfare and the public economy were allowed to expand since, far from threatening the market economy, it actually made things easier for industry. The development followed modern economic theories that the growth in the market economy, with its consequent movement of population, centralisation, impoverishment of work, declining local environments, was 'necessary' if the welfare system was to be built up.

Welfare in crisis

At the same time we know that the market economy is experiencing a series of recurring international crises. These crises and the demand for profit have forced through further rationalisation and calls for even greater efficiency. The mobility of the work force has brought about great and comprehensive changes in living conditions. People have had to move throughout the whole of the industrial period. Society has accepted this development, and its aim has sometimes even been to make this mobility in the labour market run as smoothly as possible.

The development of social welfare has brought us great improvements in material and social security. Better housing, more nursery schools, better medical care and a better service for the handicapped and the elderly. At the same time the development has been characterised by disaffection, loss of sociability and a feeling of impotence. As long as we were convinced that the development meant progress we could overlook the disadvantages.[8] We believed that social problems were the price we had to pay for the 'right' development. Industry demanded more efficiency, higher profits, large-scale operations. Rationalisation, computerisation, staff mobility continued. At the same time the public sector also increased. We can speak of a *public revolution* not only in connection with expenditure but in the form of the powerful society's institutions and authorities. In many ways the public economy seemed to model itself on the market economy. The market's models of efficiency 'spilled over' into the public sector. We got large hospitals, large effective schools and a large scale generally. The large society is acquiring increasing power over our everyday existence.

But the strong society did not become a society where everyone felt responsibility, influence and participation. Social community spirit, everyday solidarity have not been developed. It increasingly became the role of the state in the post-war period to intervene in an attempt to modify and solve social problems caused by the market economy, but an increasing number of people were at the same time beginning to question the perfection of the welfare state, the sweeping changes with, on the one hand, improvements in the family's material conditions, better housing, more nursery schools, better medical care, service for the handicapped, etc, and on the other hand, alarm at increased disaffection, apathy, impotence and a lack of community spirit—the welfare state's 'hangover'. The symptoms were increasing problems between young people and their parents, and a loss of the ability to understand other people's social situation, an ability which is a basic essential if there is to be any solidarity among people.[10]

When you are a child you're wrapped in cotton wool, then the cotton wool is suddenly torn away, and you stand there cold and frozen in a hard world and don't know what to do with yourself. A lot of people start on drugs. For most of them things go wrong at home. It is better if you can look at reality from the beginning so that you can learn. If parents quarrel they should say to their children that they shouldn't take it personally. Say 'It isn't your fault'. Often you think: what have I done now? What are they quarrelling for?

Pia, aged 14

Caring as a profession

In order to deal with increasing social problems the social sector has been further expanded. This has meant among other things that a number of duties that people could have done themselves, as voluntary unpaid work, have been transferred to remunerated public work. There is a strong tendency towards professionalisation and services in the social sector, especially in areas affecting children.

Social care has, in many respects, been taken over by society's various institutions.

The changes in care are closely associated with the growing demands of industrialism. Care has, of tradition, been maintained mainly by the women of the households. Before industrialism this happened in more open, broad social contexts where the family and the household played a large part. Industrialism has caused the family to unite in a more intimate relationship. The immediate public are excluded and responsiblity for the care of children and the elderly is increasingly the duty of the mother alone. It is striking how the *state's* interest in public care is now keeping pace with the gradually mounting demand for married women in the labour market.

There was a great demand for female labour in the 1950s and 1960s. Women and adolescents for a long time constituted a reserve work force. In the period of growth and the boom economy, industry became very interested in them. In times of recession and economic crisis they were thrown into unemployment. In this situation it can again become important to emphasise the significance of all *mothers* staying at home with their children. That we discuss here the shortcomings in society's care of children and the elderly does not imply such a view of the woman's role; on the contrary, everybody has the right to paid employment, but as we shall show in a later chapter, *everybody* has also the right, both men and women, to share in caring work. Although women were taken into paid employment, society did not arrange adequate care for children and the elderly. The unpaid work which women had previously carried out, became neglected. It is striking how women's contributions to caring have been underestimated. Institutions have had difficulty in creating a system of care for children and the elderly which matches the women's efforts. It is also worth noting that even when women are professionally employed they also have to assume a great deal of responsiblity for care in the home. Many women have to do two jobs, one paid, the other in the home, and live with the perpetual fear that they will not be able to cope with both.

Hand in hand with expanded caring services have come new professional bodies, responsible for care. Care is a comprehensive term for a series of activities, all aimed at preventing people from falling out of the community.[11] Efforts have to be concentrated on situations and conditions where this risk is great, such as, for example, when we are young, old, ill, have psychological troubles, where there is abuse, etc. The purpose of care is then to keep the individual within the community. But is this something that scientifically trained experts are better at than ordinary people? If the community and care are to work there must be a network of people willing to get involved. The question is what happens when the only network is maintained by salaried staff in the public sector service system.

Expert knowledge versus everyday competence

The professions are trained to 'take care' of people's ordinary problems. There is a risk that professionalisation will lead to monopoly and compartmentalisation. There is a widening gap between expert knowledge and everyday knowledge in the relations between the 'carers' and children. Progress has, without doubt, contributed to increased insight into children's development and needs, but parents' uncertainty about rearing their children and their relationship with them, has also increased. The everyday competence which had governed contacts between parents, other adults and children has been called into question. While parents have less and less time to be together with their children, the children, to a corresponding degree, have been fostered by society's trained staff. Facts about children and their lives are compiled within professional circles.

For people outside those circles this development has often led to competence gained by other means being rejected as a basis for child care. Theories on child rearing fluctuate from day to day and confusion is sometimes compounded when one expert contradicts another. The parents' self-confidence is diminished. Fearing to repeat the mistakes made by their own parents, they discard well-tried experiences which could have been useful and rely instead on the experts. Half-digested theories become rules for life.[12]

You always hear, 'you're old enough to know better'. And then the next day, 'you can't do that, you're only a child'. You're stuck between two worlds the whole time, the world of the child and the world of the adult. Sometimes all you want to do is get a flat of your own, as soon as possible, where you know you can be completely on your own, with nobody bothering about what you're doing. Some place you can creep into, a little den, and hide. Sometimes you have one of those difficult patches. You just want to be left in peace but everybody runs after you, corrects you the whole time, nags you for being what you are.

Pia, aged 14

Professionalising social care is also connected with our increasing tendency to take our arguments from science. Step by step, a new attitude towards expert knowledge, which controls and directs people's daily lives, is gaining ground. Workers' lives on the shop floor, children's schools, maternity care, home design, sexuality in the family, the aims of leisure, are all being moulded by scientific argument. In this way science is helping to preserve the myth that social problems are not connected with politics and the organisation of society and that trained professionally active people are needed to tackle everyday problems.

Another defect of this professionalisation is our growing dependence on state support and on experts, for survival when we are ill or have social problems, for rearing our children or tending the elderly. We can speak of a social service mentality that has grown up out of the powerful welfare machine and contrasts strongly with the popular movements' ideologies about involvement. Service and professionalisation give us a false security. We rely so heavily on the different professions or on 'the state' solving our problems that we don't even bother to try to understand matters concerning health. We don't feel we can involve ourselves in the social problems that arise around us, since we 'haven't a clue'. This can lead to a dangerous passivity and dependence. Dependence impoverishes the capacity for self help in a social environment and people's ability to take care of their own and other people's problems. If you come across disorderly alcoholics or the neighbourhood's young trouble-makers, it is easier to call in the police or the social authorities, rather than to do something about it yourself.

3   Living in no-man's-land

Our description of how conditions have changed for children and adolescents is important for an appreciation of what it is like to be young today. We shall now look more closely at some of the menacing images that young people today have to live with. We must remember, however, that not all young people suffer equally from the trends we shall illustrate. We begin by describing adolescence as a protracted interval between childhood and adulthood, when one seems to be living in a vacuum. This vacuum is made worse by adults fearing to exert influence and by the division between children and adults. A serious feature is children's lack of faith in the future. We also look at new menaces which can influence the formation of the ego. Finally we deal with the drastic cultural change which has made most children and adolescents passive onlookers in society.

Adolescence is introduced

The rapid break-up of a recognised social order and the questioning of hitherto accepted norms led to self-doubt and uncertainty about the importance of age, sex and class, about right and wrong, about nature and culture. Nor were the members of the family united any longer in common work which placed them in meaningful relationships to each other. Fathers could no longer guide their sons in the skills of farming and handicraft. The men were separated from the home's production unit and its social life. The father was absent more and more from the family and therefore from the children's daily life. His work and function were unseen and abstract. These new fathers became 'spare-time dads'. The relation between man/husband and woman/wife also changed from working together to being together during their leisure time. Today we can almost talk of a fatherless culture, where many children grow up without close daily contact with adult males.[1]

We have already described how childhood was 'invented'. A further period of dependence was then added. Adolesence, free from responsibility, can be called a protracted interlude, a lengthy period of immaturity and minority, between the games of childhood and the demands of adult life.[2]

As adolescence begins to be seen as a special period in life there is growing concern about how this stage should be developed.[3] Adolescence is also burdened with special characteristics, such as rebellion and unwillingness to work. People talk problems of adolesence: these problems are increasingly described in psychological terms without reference to the role of the surrounding community. Adolescents are singled out as a 'problem class' in society. One begins to discern a special adolescent culture. The generation gap and the opposition towards adult culture are taken to be basic features of this adolescent culture. What was more, apprehensions could be 'proved' by the first youth disturbances in the cities, for instance the so-called 'Götgata riots' in Stockholm at the end of the 1940s.

Various youth groups in 'danger zones' for crime and addiction had to be protected from harm by the efforts of schools and through leisure activities. These leisure activities also have a philanthropic origin. At the outset voluntary forces from the upper and middle classes—clergymen, teachers, army officers and doctors—helped the adolescents. For these groups, 'saving' the adolescents was an aim that gave purpose to their lives. The youth pastors' 'mission' among adolescents who were roaming the streets and those who were prostitutes in the 1940s, is one example. The psychological view of adolescence and middle-class ideology were united in these first efforts at communal youth and leisure activities. The local authorities subsequently accepted increasing responsibility for the activities. Youth clubs combined the psychological view and middle-class ideology. The clubs would gather up these straying, unattached adolescents off the streets, and almost literally channel them via the clubs' cafés and group activities into societies. Soon education makes its entrance. Trained youth leaders take over from the first idealistic enthusiasts. They would now professionally stimulate meaningful leisure activities, principally hobbies and other occupations. A whole new local authority sector sprang up in the 1950s and 60s—the leisure sector—administered by local councils where youth clubs became the foundation stone. Into the bargain we get new professional groups, youth leaders, leisure instructors, leisure experts, leisure leaders, etc. All with the job of dealing with adolescents.

A vacuum of leisure

In today's chaos of values, norms, morals (or lack of them) and a strong sense of conflict between ideals and reality, many children and adolescents are vulnerable and exposed. They are vulnerable not least because the teens are normally a time of doubt, of severing close ties, of uncertainty and of searching for identity. The teens are 'the moment of truth', when a series of conscious and unconscious conflicts are aired and appraised. Relations with both parents and the environment are at stake. Adolescence is a time of severing close ties and a time of searching for a platform to stand on—an identity of one's own. The teenager is looking for a place in society. At the same time, he/she is trying to understand himself/herself as an individual, life itself, to find his/her own lifestyle, something to believe in, values to live by, in short a *raison d'être*. This is a natural process, an assertion of one's own will and it often contains elements of unease, confusion and aggression which many adults react against strongly. The break creates a condition of confusion, a feeling of *living in no-man's-land*.[4]

Children and adolescents today are cut off from productive paid work. There is no place for them in the entire work for the common welfare. Instead they are left to their own devices in an environment with a surplus of people of their own age. Their potential is not being used—in the housing area they only get in the way. Adolescents lack contact with adults.[5] They are not given responsiblity for others, they don't do work that is necessary for other people. They are held in an extended *hiatus* between childhood and adulthood.[6] They have landed in a *vacuum of leisure* which waits only to be filled.

I flit about like a bird, you might say. If anybody were to ask me what I was doing last week I'd hardly ever remember.

It's always different. So many new things are always happening.

If you don't want to stay in, you can't just be out in town hanging around.

If I've decided to stay at home one evening and I hear they're playing at the Palais, I say to myself, 'No, I'm not going.' By nine o'clock there seems so much pressure on me. Half of me wants to go, the other half doesn't. I often do go out in the end.

Pia, aged 14

Lack of ideology

The climate of ideological debate changed drastically during the post-war period, not least during the cold war. All the energies of social reform went towards building a strong society, which would give people security, welfare and social services. Many people also reacted against the old society and the ideological oppression of fascism. Criticism of all forms of authority was severe.[7] Openness and neutral values were now advocated which in their practical application resulted in a lack of guidelines in relationships between children and their guardians. Those now growing up are in many ways 'freed' from the guidance involved in upbringing. Upbringing is increasingly released from its original form and is dealt with less by people for whom children have an emotional and involved attachment.[8] Nor is its point of departure communal work and participation in production. It is increasingly private and idealistic.

Schools were to be objective and factual. Knowledge was objective whilst politics were 'dangerous'. In practice this meant that the knowledge conveyed by schools bore the stamp of upper- and middle-class values, language and culture.

Nor have children been able to encounter ideological values in youth organisations. Youth organisations' activities were also to be neutral. In the 1950s, for instance, political and religious youth organisations were not awarded the new official grants to leisure groups.[9] This meant that youth organisations' activities were for a long time characterised by practical occupations rather than the ideological training that was so important when popular movements were first started.

The home too was to be free from ideological influences. Parents did not believe they should exert influence, a thought which ran contrary to that of the parents in the early popular movements who recognised the need to train children politically, ideologically and morally. Children were now to be free to choose their ideology from a host of values, or else the training was handed over to the professions.

This lack of ideology was also encouraged by many parents' fear of taking an ideological upbringing seriously; by the new child professionals' rejection of ideological training; the reaction to the fascist training of the war; the belief in the scientific ideals of neutrality and objectivity; making adolescence a psychological problem; youth revolt; local councils' incipient interest in doing something for young people. All this was combined in a view of adolescence as a time to be filled with the completion of semi-manufactured goods.

The young generation is increasingly encountering a society that deviates from that in which previous generations have grown up. Tradition has ceased to stake out guide lines for the individual's life. Instead, teenagers encounter many equivocal norms, value-pluralism or its opposite, a lack of norms. The adults around them feel redundant as advisers, just when teenagers need adults with whom they can identify themselves. The vacuum is being extended.

Where are the idols of everyday life?

Children and adolescents have a genuine need to develop within their own age-group. The culture of one's own age-group is essential if development into adult life is to work normally. One's own group can channel a 'healthy' revolt against the dominance of the adult world. Perhaps one of the great disadvantages for rural children was being constantly subject to the rules and control of authority and the adult world. Contemporary accounts, however, show that rural children also had recourse to the company of their own age-groups. But children also need to identify themselves with people in the adult world, both parents and others. They need positive, supportive adults who instruct and foster, and who dare stand by their values and convictions, adults who are not afraid to influence, who can serve as models in the search for identity. But most adults have withdrawn. Few children meet adults other than their parents And their parents have less and less time. Adolescents meet adult teachers, youth leaders, sports leaders, but they are never really important, according to the adolescents themselves.[10] Is this because their professional roles and functions are a barrier to a genuine personal relationship? But culture exists through the successful transmission of norms, values, knowledge and morals. The ideal state of affairs is surely one where there are good everyday, natural contacts and practical co-operation between children and adults and where there are also opportunities to develop the culture of one's own age-group.

Segregating childhood from adult life creates disturbing features which affect the quality of the whole of society.

Children feel the need for adult contacts. Youth surveys show that children are often materially satisfied but socially starved. Often a pet, or the dream of owning one's own pet, compensates for the lack of social contacts.[11] Our children and adolescents buy and own quite a lot of belongings; however, when we ask them which of the things they possess is their favourite, they nearly always mention an adult, with whom they can have a social relationship, grandmother, grandfather, brother, cousin or an animal. Relationships are more important than possessions. As a child, one has, for better or worse, a relationship with other people, not least with adults. In this way children, too, become a kind of social attribute. But interviews with young people show, both directly and 'between the lines', the picture of a society where the adult generation, to an increasing extent, chooses to live without children.

This too reinforces the vacuum.

Really when you reach your twenties and wonder about having children, perhaps then you don't dare. You never know what they'll be coming to. And they've started with computerised music. Computers do everything twice as fast and twice as well as humans. That's the sort of thing you get scared of, that the computer will take over.

Pia, aged 14

We have to set limits

Children are not happy without the limits which emerge from natural co-operaton between the generations.

We repeat actions which lead to our needs being fulfilled. There must be some kind of equilibrium between various needs on the one hand, and the possibility of satisfying those needs on the other. Our needs, basic or cultivated, can be unpredictable and insatiable. If there is no outside force limiting them they can become a source of torment and trouble for us. Nor can available means be sufficient to satisfy our needs, if there are no limits. Satisfaction is only possible where desires and needs are limited. In a society where these limits do not operate there is free scope. The social rules have gone out of action. We are all left to our own devices, there is no solidarity. It is difficult to get your bearings. It is a well known fact that we easily feel sick or lose our balance and control of our faculties if we find ourselves in a place where we cannot get our usual bearings. We lose our footing and our focal-point. Metaphorically speaking our society is close to that state of disorientation and passivity.[13]

The absence of boundaries increases the vacuum.

Little faith in the future

Against this background we must also look at many adolescents' lack of faith in the future, their pessimism and disappointment. Our youth surveys alarm us on several points and perhaps most of all when we speak to children about the future. Not that they lack visions of how it could be. If it were up to the children we would have a world without war, with less traffic, a world where children are 'seen', a world where children and adults spend more time together. In general children do not believe their dream will come true. Instead they are extremely uneasy and often afraid. They almost revel in the science-fiction-like horror that is to come. Girls are more troubled and dissappointed than boys. They are afraid of war, the destruction of the environment, traffic and a technology that they do not think man can control. Boys are more 'conditioned'. They think, admittedly, that mankind is going to the dogs, but that they themselves will no doubt manage.

I actually think there'll be a third world war. And it won't be so much a war as a massacre, the whole thing. Unless there's a miracle, a complete reversal. . . .

Göran, aged 18

Sometimes I think—just what on earth is going to happen. Heavens, if I live long enough to have a child and a job, and all that. How will it be . . . ? Personally I think there'll be another world war. I just hope it won't be in my life-time.

Marja, aged 17

The Me Decade

The drastic changes in society have influenced the conditions of children's upbringing in different ways. Many researchers think that the changes have had social and psychological consequences. They have affected the formation of the individual ego.

A society that loses its faith in the future and at the same time denies its historical identity cannot transmit its culture,[15] for that requires co-operation between the generations. Rural children established their ties with previous generations through social conditions. It is different today. Those who were there before us are quickly forgotten and we know nothing about those who will come after us. There is a danger that individuals today are losing the ability to feel historical continuity, the feeling of being a link between the generations, of bearing traces of what has been and what will be. Every society *reproduces* or transmits its culture, its norms, in the individual in the forming of the personality. In a society where children's resources are not utilised, where children and adults are segregated, where children are left in a vacuum and a period of waiting, this reproduction finds itself in a deep crisis which in the long run can threaten our whole culture.

One way of reacting against the social and cultural changes is self-absorption, ie *narcissism*.[16] Narcissus was the handsome Greek youth who according to myth was so infatuated by his own image and so frustrated at not being able to possess himself that he pined away and was transformed into a narcissus flower. Narcissism is a natural condition in both children and adults. When the child is building up its ego it looks for its mirror image. There is also a hint of narcissism in all adult love. It is normal to love oneself as one would ideally like to be. Freud called it the ideal ego. A strong ego is important, but we must also love others. We become ill if we cannot, or are not allowed to love others. The new narcissism is an inflated self-love which the absence of social interdependence has prevented from developing into love of others. Its most prominent feature is that people do not believe that they can change their lives or conditions in any decisive area. They have persuaded themselves instead that it is self-realisation which is significant. It is more important to take care of yourself, your personal development, to build up your body, devote yourself to therapy, to dancing and consuming. Those who do not believe society has any future consider it better to live for the moment, not for ancestors or descendants. The cultural ideal which emerges emphasises the importance of living for yourself, here and now.

Withdrawal into the cult of one's own personality is one of many reactions to the problems we face in today's society. It is not only connected with self-love and selfishness in the traditional sense (people have always been selfish) but stems from particular changes in our society and our culture-bureaucracy, therapeutic ideologies, the rationalisations of our inner lives, separations, changes in family life, patterns of specialisation and consumer culture, increased unemployment, rejection, the destruction of the environment, adolescents' vulnerability, etc. In industry the demands for specialisation and computerisation have meant that people are unable to influence work processes. This makes reality seem unsatisfactory. It nourishes restlessness and a need for compensation. With these conditions in mind the new personality traits are an understandable way of reacting to social changes.

Thus we develop a psychological defence against strong personal and emotional relationships and instead we increasingly surround ourselves with a protective superficiality. The flight from strong emotions is justified as emotional liberation. The need for freedom is emphasised strongly in all relationships. At its most extreme the spirit of free will is an absence of obligations, and its result is often ruthlessness. When we are dissatisfied with personal relationships, we tend not to trust too much in love or friendship. We avoid dependence on others and allow no demands on personal relationships. Personal relationships become superficial and unsatisfactory. Instead we live for the moment. But in a life without an awareness of limits or boundaries, a dependence on incidental forces is built up with consequent personal crises. The narcissist's misfortune is that he cannot be dependent on other people. He has to reassure himself constantly in a mirror-image conveyed by the people around him. His apparent freedom does not permit him to shine alone in the light of his individualism. He can overcome his insecurity only by seeing his grandiose ego reflected in the care and admiration of others. People and the world become a mirror.

We dream of fame and glamour, we identify ourselves with stars and famous personalities and despise the ordinary. We restlessly seek the emotional titillations of the moment. We are promiscuous in our sexual relationships as a defence against emotional attachments and intimacy. Instead we seek sex without emotional engagement. The dream of sexual licence is also legitimised as sexual freedom. We are afraid of growing old and of death and are abnormally worried about our health, and this attracts us to therapy and therapeutuic groups. It becomes increasingly difficult to accept everyday banalities. Egocentricity gives a vicarious warmth — an illusion that one can flee from everyday life.

The far-reaching changes in society have created completely new patterns of socialisation. Growing specialisation of economic and social functions has deprived the family of its economic, protective and child-rearing role. The family's part in the child's upbringing has receded proportionately as playschool, television and school have taken more and more of its training. The result is the child's diminished ability to recognise and reflect itself in its parents and other adults it admires. Instead the influence of the *peer group* increases[17] and begins to function as a 'social womb', an incubator, and as a protection against future demands from outside. Through the peer group one can escape from the outside world and at the same time gain self-confirmation.

Somebody I know I like and who likes me. Then at least I know there's somebody, somebody in this world who likes me besides my parents. Somebody outside. That's what I think.

Pia, aged 14

The worst thing that could happen to me would be being left all alone in the world. Losing all my friends. I think that would be awful — being excluded.

Marja, aged 17

From participant to onlooker

The welfare and social security system we have built up is of such a nature that an increasing number of people, especially children and adolescents, are left without responsibility, role or function. Most of them are not involved in working for the welfare system, can not, or feel that they cannot, influence the course it takes. 'We don't decide the future.' — 'We just have to accept it and be grateful to others.' Being an onlooker instead of a participant is a drastic cultural change which 'children of the state' have been made to feel. The rural child was at least a participant in the local community, even if it did live a hard and poor life. The state child could reach twenty-five without ever having produced anything of use to himself or anybody else or having shown concern for others.[18]

As long as social development was progressing, industry was growing and there were still the funds for social reforms, optimism could be maintained, but the economic crises of the last few years have revealed that something has gone wrong. Anger has found an outlet in riots or a depressing passivity, in the abuse of drugs, or in consumption. There are many ways of reacting to the conflict between ideals and reality. Adolescents between fifteen and twenty-five are the group which has perhaps felt the great changes in social development most intensely. As a group, they have perhaps had to sustain most of the cultural conflicts in society, since they have still not found a safe basis for the problems and conflicts which have emerged in our society. They suffer greatly by the distance between recognised ideals and the reality they encounter. For the whole of the postwar period we have been striving for a society with these recognised ideals: equality, equal values, fellowship, security, responsibility, progress and a purpose in life. The conflict lies in the fact that many adolescents daily experience the opposite of these ideals. They see a society where there is a great inequality, especially in the economic field. They see a society where people's isolation has increased. They feel that they and their friends are useless. There is no place for them in production. They know that many of them will not get jobs when they leave school or that they have already been rejected while at school. Many adolescents live in real insecurity. They live in a society which will not give them responsibility and the result is a structural passivity, or rebellion.[19]

In 1980–1, many European cities again experienced so-called youth riots, with house occupations and street fighting which society tried to quell by severe measures (Berlin, Liverpool). One typical way of reacting to social conflicts is aggression and violence. Another is an escape from the problems through speed and excitement, or alcohol

and drugs. Many adolescents try to resolve the conflicts in a way acceptable to society, such as finding their way to youth organisations, etc. Others find this is useless. They withdraw into passivity or they devote all their energies to their close group and use their time and attention in acquiring possessions. It becomes a substitute for human involvement.

I grew up with a class mate who is on his way to sheer hell now. He started glue-sniffing in the second form, playing truant in the third form and started to smoke hash in the fourth form. Now he's on powder and all that. I saw him in town a few weeks ago. It nearly makes you weep to look at him. When you know he used to be just like yourself. His eyes are all over the place and you nearly have to write things down to get him to grasp anything. He just sits there looking like a wreck.

Göran, aged 18

The dual effects of social development, the revolution in material welfare and at the same time the hollowing out of children's and adolescents' role, function and value in society, are the cause of the vacuum, the waiting period. Mobility, social and cultural changes, professionalisation, value pluralism, segregation of children and adults, the crumbling of limits to our actions, fear of influencing and making demands, have reinforced the vacuum. A weak ego is a further socio-psychological factor in the understanding of how youth culture can make its mark commercially. We shall now see how the child of the state becomes the 'child of the market'.

4 The market turns to children

In this chapter we shall scrutinise the market's relation to children. We shall see how the market turns to children and offers them a new function in society – the role of consumer. We shall first examine the historical development of the market economy, the background to its dominance in our society. Children are an important consumer group and the commercialised child and youth culture is the market's 'gift' to its children, whom it educates with its content and values. Many people wonder why commercial youth culture is so attractive. We shall try to answer that question with the aid of theories about children's need for fantasy, emotional experiences and identification. In one section we examine how the market distributes its goods and services through advertising. Finally we illustrate the counter-cultures and counter-forces which, despite everything, exist in children's own culture.

From family economy to market revolution

Changes in living patterns are closely connected with how we organise the economy, production and reproduction. In Sweden, as in many other countries, the market economy has unmistakably come to play the largest part in this context. The market economy has its own history. In different periods the market has increased its power over our lives. To understand its dominance better we shall, in this section, examine its development.

In the pre-industrial society, i.e. before the nineteenth century, households were the centres of both productive and reproductive work. We can speak of a household or *family economy*. With a cash economy and industrialisation, an increasing number of men and unmarried women took on paid employment. We get a more clearcut division between owners and non-owners, between those who own the means of production and those who sell their labour. The market economy, the system based on buying and selling, expands in step with the industrial development.

An expanding market favours specialisation and the disciplining of labour. One has to work co-ordinated periods and leave the home for certain periods. Time is money. Initially it was the men who went out to paid employment to support the family. The women were responsible for the unpaid work, connected with the household and the home. Working in premises at a distance from the home marks the dividing line between paid and unpaid employment, between 'production' and 'reproduction'. Goods produced for home consumption were neither produced on a large scale nor sold on the market. As a result it was no longer considered real work. Unpaid employment was downgraded and unnoticed.

In the early period of industrialism, i.e. the beginning of the nineteenth century, men's wages were not sufficient to support the family. The elderly, women and children all sold their labour in the labour market and so contributed to the necessities of life. In this *family-wage economy,* people were forced to work from dawn to dusk in workshops, mills, match factories, glassworks, mines etc.

Gradually the ideal developed that married women, even in the working classes, should look after the home and the children whilst the family lived on the husband's wages. But working-class women still worked as maids, cleaners, washerwomen, seamstresses and in textile, food, tobacco or clothes factories. However, many working women gave up their paid employment completely when they got married and had children.

With new efficient production methods and technological changes, the elderly and children were no longer profitable to industry. Because of their contribution in the home, women, too, were treated separately in the labour market. But the development led, at the same time, to improved living standards and drove back poverty. There was a transition to a *family consumer economy*. Families could afford to spend money on the home, hygiene, furniture, pleasant furnishings and eventually on leisure. Family life changed in character from a production unit to a consumption unit. Child and adolescent contributions to the unpaid work in the household no longer counted. Children were left to their games, and adolescents had to devote their time to preparing for the future in school.

The great economic boom after the Second World War also led to a shortage of labour, and the expansion of the public sector laid the foundations for a *family service economy*. More and more women were required in the labour force. Social reproduction increasingly becomes paid employment, sold in the labour market. The labour market has gradually changed, so that adolescents are no longer in demand. New groups of salaried workers have been trained and appointed to take charge of children and adolescents: nursery and playschool teachers, child-minders, park leaders, leisure organisers, school nurses, psychologists, specialist teachers, etc.[1]

The promise of industrialism

In Sweden the industrial revolution began in the nineteenth century. Poverty and misery were rife. Hunger, monotonous diet, overcrowding, wretched conditions of hygiene, lack of medical care and of education were problems which dominated everyday life for the majority of the population. The most essential thing was naturally to free oneself from that poverty as soon as possible and with all available means. At the end of the century, Sweden was a country with very little industry. The precursors of industry expressed the period's faith in the future. Industry promised riches and a demi-paradise. Here as in other parts of the world, industrialisation and a market economy seemed the best way of escaping poverty swiftly. Most people were agreed on that, whatever their ideological persuasions.[2]

In terms of efficiency, the industrial method of production was much superior to the old crafts. Market economy production also provided a surplus which, at least in times of a buoyant economy and after a hard political struggle, could help to solve most people's overriding problem — material poverty. Through the provision of the state, the surplus could be distributed to those most in need of support. Particularly in Sweden's postwar 'harvest' years, large resources could be set aside for social reforms. Market economy production assumed a leading position, since it resulted in a palpable and, for most people, appreciable improvement in living standards and social security.

The market revolution

The basic framework of the market economy is a commercial system of *buying and selling*. This system has developed extremely rapidly in Sweden during the twentieth century. We could almost call it a *market revolution* in the post-war period.[3] It was carried along by a new scientific research in economics, new methods of production, distribution and advertising, the need for new markets, the high standard of living and optimism about the future. The effects in industry were the large increase in scale, the demands for greater rationalisation and efficiency, a more flexible market and a new attachment to the international market.

The market continually strives to extend its boundaries and its power. It replaces the fetters of poverty with other chains. We have to pay dearly for the market having raised us out of poverty and scarcity. What we did not foresee, or where we most under-estimated the power of the market economy, was in its ability to influence and penetrate our innermost lives. The market has formed and taken over increasing areas of our lives which had not been commercialised and where it does not belong. People's everyday existence has been led more and more into this 'buy and sell' mentality. It affects human relations, relationships between children and adults and family life generally. Consumption is taken to be the solution to everyday problems; the market influences and fosters children's ideology.

One example of these changes is seen in the way people more and more frequently assume they will be paid for what they do for others. More and more deeds and acts are being valued in money. Our research shows, for instance, that children today get paid for work that would previously have been a natural part of the home's production and work.[4] They are paid for cutting the grass, doing the shopping, minding their young brothers and sisters, cleaning their room etc. They negotiate for as much as they can get for these jobs so that they can buy consumer goods, which are a 'must'.[5] It appears that in difficult economic times the children most often come first. It is particularly common for a single parent to make personal sacrifices to enable the children to buy things they need, want or which their friends have.

The new 'child jobs' and wages are, of course, part of the parents' economic training of their children, but can also be an example of how the market's laws about everything having to be valued in money terms are eating deep into the family's private life and reaching an ever younger age group.

The market's weaknesses

A series of weaknesses, which affect our lives, are built into the market economy system. The market economy is characterised, for instance, by recurring international crises which entail economic stagnation, a break in the rate of growth and significant unemployment. The economic crises of the past few years have been more serious and have gone deeper than for many years. One of the main principles of the market economy is the need for growth, but there are important social limits to this growth in the prevailing market economy. There are, beyond these limits, a multitude of unsolved problems which the market economy is not able to solve. The market is based on a *scarcity economy*.[6] Goods and services are, in general, of value only to a few financially powerful people. At the same time the market wants to expand and provide goods valuable to the other section of the population. When a large section of the population has reached a position similar to that of the financially powerful, however, the latter must seek new goods and services, which are exclusive to them. Scarcity economy encourages a perpetual climbing and a dissatisfaction with the present position. One must try to keep ahead of everyone else, or at least ahead of a group which has been defined as being inferior to one's own. Ideas on equality of resources and supply threaten the market. In a global perspective this competition for scarce resources can increase the differences in material standards between rich and poor countries. Greater economic growth in itself has not shown therefore that it can reduce the gaps between rich and poor. On the other hand, what we call negative growth in a market economy like ours has shown that it widens the gaps in society.[7]

A common economic theory assumes that we need strong economic growth within the market economy to achieve a sufficient surplus to deal with the increased social problems, i.e. growth is essential for a sound public sector. But of course it could also be argued that increased economic growth cannot be achieved without further rationalisation, efficiency, mobility, the removal of those who cannot cope with the competition, increased addiction which causes the community unnecessarily high social costs which in turn increases the burden on the public sector. To solve the social problems caused by growth, the public must be given additional funds, which makes demands on increased growth, etc.

The struggle for purchasing power and the search for new potential markets are typical of our market economy. The consumers must not be allowed to be satisfied, they must consume more. Goods not strictly necessary become essential, in other words a growth of *non-essentials*. The market exercises its control over our lives through inbuilt obsolescence, encouraging waste and a perpetual demand for renewal of products. Old articles 'simply must' be exchanged for new since they cannot be repaired, in other words there is an inbuilt material obsolescence. The superiority of new models is praised in huge advertising campaigns which render the previous models old fashioned and emotionally dated. This *self-perpetuating waste* is an essential component of the market revolution.

The market destroys work

The content and value of work is central to our lives. It is basic to our identity, self-esteem and development. Even if most children are not affected by paid work of their own, they are to an extremely great extent indirectly dependent on their parents' working conditions. Work is part of the living pattern of human beings. In this sense, work is a cultural process. Work affects the total life situation of an individual. Work is rich in content if it demands thought and independence. Such work teaches the individual that he/she can cope with difficulties and problems outside work too. Conversely, work without such content can affect the whole social environment. It can lead to disillusion, passivity and a diminished ability to question one's own life situation. Thought, action and responsibility are, or ought to be, inextricably combined in work. This affords job-satisfaction and develops the whole personality. When work functions as it should, one should be able to utilise one's skills and knowledge.

The market economy's implacable governing of the content of work has caused far-reaching changes for the individual, for better or worse.[8] Most industrial jobs have become easier, but we cannot deny that work has become impoverished. The most efficient work has been designed with the help of science. The effects on creative work, work as a cultural process, are serious. Skill used to lie at the very heart of one's work. Craftsmen used to combine *hand and head*. In modern management techniques, there has been a strategy of separating hand from head. 'Taylorism' suggested that work should be seen as a necessary evil, a burden, rather than a cultural process. Workers did not need work satisfaction. The central issue was, instead, one of earnings. The workers should find 'self realisation' *outside* their work and should escape from work as soon as possible. Leisure becomes life itself.[10]

Satisfaction and compensation are to be found through consumption in one's leisure time and in the home. In his private life, the individual is expected to consume the goods produced by the system. By tending and repairing his capacity for work, on the one hand, so that production can continue, and continually demanding and consuming goods and services, on the other, he helps to perpetuate the market. Food and sleep can be compensated for individually, but emotional and psychological strains can be compensated for only together with other people, in the family, with a partner or with a group of friends. The small isolated nuclear family of today is therefore of increasing importance in just this context. It is a kind of 'filling station' where the individual always requires a topping up of emotional and social contacts after having being drained at work.[11] But the 'new' family is no safe port in a storm. Instead it is characteristic that the more the family is expected to cope with all emotional problems, the less well prepared have our privatised and isolated families become.[12]

This dual world – work and leisure – has thus permeated people's lives, both children and adults. For many people, the aim and purpose of their efforts at work is the continual improvement and development of their private living conditions. There is also a duality between production and consumption, so that in our system consumption falls into the sphere of leisure and, in that situation, performs as strong a compensatory function as possible.

There has to be leisure time consumption for the market economy to continue to grow. A high level of consumption is necessary if we are to create greater material welfare. In this way leisure becomes even more firmly anchored in our consciousness. But people are whole and indivisible – we cannot live two lives. The strains and impoverishment of work cannot be compensated in leisure time. Many of those who have strenuous, stressful, monotonous jobs find that their leisure time is wasted. At the end of a day's work, they have not the energy to spend time with their family until they have been at home for several hours.

Every day I get up at five. I'm always tired in the morning no matter when I get up, so it makes no difference that it is so early. We finish quite early instead – at three in the afternoon. My job is to smoke pork, ham and lean cuts all day – going right into an oven full of smoke, at 130°. It's nice to have got so much responsibility even though I am so young. There's a lot of money at risk every day. The meat could turn out raw or get burnt.

After a long weekend I long to get back to work. I get nervous if I haven't anything to keep my hands busy. And then I've got good workmates that I want to meet. I really look forward to seeing them again after a holiday.

Göran, aged 18

Culture becomes a commodity

The market economy's increasing power has great consequences for the whole organisation of society and therefore for children's upbringing. It means nothing less than that society and life in society is run as an appendage to the economy, to the market. Instead of the economy being governed by social relations, those relations are embedded in the economy. Social ties are eaten away. The economy is released from ancient collective obligations. Individualism is a cultural precondition for the new economic order. This involves an enormous cultural change: man is no longer seen as a part of his social role but as an individual, above and outside all social roles.[13] Money enlarges the market and destroys social harmony with the lure of freedom and enterprise. Dispersal and change are called progress. One must stand on one's own feet, hold one's own, and there is talk of independence and self-determination.[14]

The market spreads its power over the whole of our culture, stimulates the modern mass society, looks for the sale of all the goods it produces; it invests in advertising and marketing, which manipulate with the help of psychological knowledge and which systematically appeal to our weaknesses and insecurity.

Even culture is made into a consumer good. When culture is made into a commodity for mass consumption the social ties are further loosened. Whilst culture was previously transmitted and reflected in well-defined social and productive units, it has now gone up-market to be a public entity which is outside these social ties.

The market's concept of culture demands a manufactured article which can be sold on the market. This extraneous culture has increased dramatically during the past century. It is distinct from everyday culture which is sustained and created in our everyday lives.[15] In everyday culture we are principally active participants and creators, but, in the former kind, we are predominantly passive recipients and onlookers. Marketed culture in its turn is sustained by intrusive structures and is presented to us via the written word, images and sound.

Children as consumers

Children and adolescents constitute an important part of the market. They own quite a lot of clothes and leisure articles. They themselves buy a lot of them. Their income in the form of pocket money, casual work, etc, has in fact risen more quickly than normal incomes in the country. Adolescents have successfully asserted their economic position in relation to other groups in society.[16]

Different youth surveys usually show distinct differences in social groups, yet not when we compare the amount of money children from different social groups spend on consumer goods. Children from social group 3 seem to have more money at their disposal, while groups 1 and 2 are given more expensive presents from parents and other adults.[17] On the other hand there are differences in the kind of consumption among the different social groups. One study compared girls from social groups 1 and 3, for instance, and found differences in consumer habits and experiences.[18]

Boys are more materially inclined than girls. They own more and dearer goods. Their possessions are worth approximately 70 percent more than girls'. So if, for instance, girls own a 2000 kroner stereo system, the boys' will cost 3500. They are more inclined to buy more expensive articles and are more dissatisfied with their material standards.

When we asked 11-year-olds what they wanted, pets and clothes were high on the girls' list, but not on the boys'. Instead, they wanted bicycles, toys, sports equipment, i.e. more hardware. About 33 per cent of the boys followed this line. We also asked what they would like when they were older – say 15 or 16. Sixty per cent of the boys stated mopeds, motorcycles, whilst the girls (22 per cent) stuck to their pets.

Adolescents can generally name an article which they consider indispensable. 78 per cent consider, for instance, that bicycles were essential. Music and listening equipment are extremely important for most of the adolescents. Almost 80 per cent thought that shopping was fun. Most of them said that they would rather buy new expensive capital goods than cheaper, secondhand ones. When adolescents buy an article the three most important points are: the price, the appearance, and the knowledge that somebody else will approve of their purchase. This applies not least to clothing, which has an important social function. When buying a pair of jeans, half of all adolescents would rather wait until they can afford the *right* ones. As they got older adolescents grow increasingly dependent on their friends' opinions and less on their parents'.[19]

I would never dream of wearing the same trousers, same boots and the same jacket as millions of other people. I'd feel quite devastated. As if I didn't exist. I'd only be a copy of someone else.

Pia, aged 14

What, then will 16-year-olds buy for themselves now and two years hence? Girls state pets, 13 per cent of the girls as against 1 per cent of the boys, but the girls' dreams of animals are not so prominent among 16-year-olds as among 11-year-olds. It is above all girls living in flats and from social group 3 who want to buy pets.

But the girls now also often want to buy clothes, 14 per cent. This wish is three times as common in social group 1 as in group 3. Over 20 per cent were thinking of investing in stereos, videorecorders, etc, more boys than girls. That, too, was slightly more common in group 1. Mopeds, motorcycles and cars on the other hand were a more common wish among boys of social group 3, 30 per cent as against 14 per cent of boys in social group 1. Adolescents from social group 1 wanted sports equipment twice as often as those in social group 3, and boys twice as often as girls. New furniture was a wish that occurred, above all, in social group 1.

What were they thinking of getting in a few years' time? 50 per cent of the girls and 75 per cent of the boys intend to buy a car. Twenty per cent of the girls as against only 7 per cent of the boys are thinking of getting a flat. Girls stated, three times as often as boys, that they were intending to get a driving licence – the boys presumably took it for granted that they would get one.

We asked the adolescents what they buy on a normal day. Among the 11-year-olds, sweets and soft drinks are predominant. Children living in flats bought more of these goods than those in villas. Most of the 11-year-olds spent five kronor or less per week on confectionery. Those who spend more, about ten to fifteen kronor a week, were generally from families living in flats. Here, therefore, the 'flat children' differed from the 'villa children'.

Clothes, dancing, travel — some examples

Sixteen-year-olds spend most money on clothes. More girls than boys would spend some money on clothes, during one month; 95 per cent of the girls as against 85 per cent of the boys. Girls are more fashion conscious than boys. Half of all boys do not really know what the latest fashion is. Only 16 per cent of the girls show the same ignorance. Among those who did know, there was great agreement as to what the latest fashion was. In the autumn of 1979, when the study was made, it was baggy clothes, baggy trousers, breeches and old men's jeans. Almost twice as many girls as boys had also bought what they considered to be 'in'; 58 per cent of girls as against 25 per cent of boys.

Adolescents are very interested in dancing. They get to know other adolescents and have a good time through dancing. Those who go to dances most often are found among adolescents who live in flats (16-year-olds). Adolescents who live in villas/terraced houses went dancing less frequently. The boys went out more seldom than the girls. Most of them thought that going out dancing was worth the money.

What do 16-year-olds do in the summer before leaving the fifth year and ending their compulsory schooling? Half of them go abroad. It was above all adolescents from social group 1 who could travel abroad. Social group 3 went abroad least. Western Europe and the United States are popular destinations. Going on a charter flight is still above all social group 1's method of going on holiday. Twenty-three per cent of the adolescents from social group 1 have been on a charter flight, as opposed to 8 per cent of social group 3. It is also more common for adolescents from group 1 to spend the summer holiday with their parents, in their own summer cottage or a rented one; about 40 per cent as against 30 per cent in social groups 2 and 3.

If the neighbour buys a new stereo, we have to buy a new stereo too. Because they can't go one better than us. If anyone buys something, others are jealous. It's the same thing with this video. Now it's as popular as hell. As soon as there's a new gadget everyone's got to buy one.

Bosse, aged 16

Children as consumers

In our society children are taught and trained to be consumers. The process which children go through when developing consumer skills, attitudes and behaviour is a gradual development or *consumer socialisation.*[20]

The commercial system consists of buying and selling. For the individual this means that he/she sells his/her labour and thereby acquires the means of consumption. Children function in this same way from an early stage. We have seen how 11-year-olds get paid for various household chores or receive pocket money. Often the pocket money is related to some achievement. Good behaviour and good school results often lead to a higher income. Nor is it unusual for children to have a spare-time job in the open market. In the higher age-groups spare-time jobs are very common.

Children soon develop a commercial interest. They are often taken shopping with their parents and are then given, or buy, small items like comics, sweets, soft drinks, etc. Half of the 11-year-olds have bought something 'yesterday' and about 20 per cent of the 16-year-olds have spent at least half an hour of their free time going around the shops 'yesterday'. Obviously this must be seen in relation to other activities which took up more of their leisure time.

Buying and consuming thus becomes a leisure activity even if that activity figures quite low on the list of activities which occupy their leisure time. About 17 per cent of the 16-year-olds spend about *half an hour* or more 'yesterday' shopping, i.e. any ordinary weekday. A good 50 per cent however, bought *something* 'yesterday'. This pattern agrees well with what we found among the 11-year-olds. Watching television, listening to music, being together with friends or parents/brothers and sisters, reading newspapers or books, doing homework or studying obviously occupies most of their afternoons and evenings. Seventy-seven per cent of the boys and 67 per cent of the girls said that they had watched television for half an hour or longer 'yesterday evening'.

Material saturation

How do the adolescents themselves view their economic standards? The answers are surprising and call for consideration. About 90 per cent say that they have sufficient money to get by on. The boys were slightly more dissatisfied than the girls, even though they had more money to spend and owned more and dearer objects than the girls. The 16-year-olds also seemed satisfied with their economic standards, even if the figure was somewhat lower (just over 70 per cent). The boys were still more dissatisfied than the girls.

The tendencies shown in the answers are interesting. Most of the children and adolescents seemed relatively satisfied with their own material standards and also with the standard attained in the country generally. The interviews concerning children's and adolescents' view of the future[21] showed that the adolescents believe we have reached a ceiling in the development of our standards, and in general they were also satisfied with that. One might well ask if this is not a relatively new historical phenomenon in the country.

Do the answers imply that the children and adolescents are materially satiated? Several of the answers in our survey suggest that they are. To a question about what the adolescents liked to do best when they get home from school in the afternoon, only about 4 per cent stated that playing with their things was the most fun. Instead social intercourse with their friends was more important.

To another question about what adolescents preferred of all they owned, most of them mentioned quite different things from gadgets and consumer goods. Instead most of them chose people in their immediate environment. It was, moreover, common for the children, especially the girls, to prefer their pets. Sixty-eight per cent of all the children had access to pets at home.

It seems to be important in these age-groups to have someone to take care of and be particularly fond of. Pets can act as a connecting link in the family. When the various members of the family come home from their various activities, the parents from work and the children from school, the pets are welcoming beings. We suspect also that the pets quite often act as a substitute 'baby sitter' in families with child care difficulties. If there is a pet at home when the children come home from school, they will not feel so lonely.

Girls especially do not lose their interest in pets, even in the higher age-groups. When, for instance, we asked the children what they wanted for Christmas or their birthday, etc, animals often cropped up again in the form of horses or dogs. There would be even more pets in the family if children had their way and if parents did not apply the brake for financial or practical reasons.

Compared with other countries it seems to be more usual for Swedish children to mention a pet when they say with whom they have the best relationship. Swedish children, therefore, differ in this from children in other countries. It is extremely unusual for children in other countries to let pets occupy such a large place in their hearts.[22]

Security cannot be bought

Our own studies, and those of others, thus give a unanimous picture. For children, contact with adults and the chance to take care of, and be responsible for, living creatures, such as a pet, is very important. Although most children have many possessions and quite a lot of money for their own use, contacts with parents and other adults and/or pets are more important than objects. Children today are materially satiated, but socially starved.

I used to sleep over in the stable when it got difficult. I took the horse blanket and gathered up some straw into a heap and lay there and cried. The horse stood with her muzzle against my tummy and nuzzled in. Then she'd lie down beside me with her head towards me. It sounds funny but I used to stand and talk to my horse. It sounds absurd: standing and discussing your problems with a horse! Even so, I think it did me more good than just crying to somebody who only stands and pats you on the back says 'There, there', without really meaning it. My horse knew the state of mind I was in. If I was sad she would be just as sad. She really tried to help me. I knew that she relied on me. It's difficult to explain.

Pia, aged 14

Children from the working class have in general more money to spend and they buy slightly more than children from the upper and middle classes. Perhaps there is an underlying ideology hidden behind these results, that our children will *have an easier time than we had,* that they *will not turn out like us.* This points to yet another of the main problems of commercialism. Children certainly appreciate the things they get and the money they have to spend, but apparently they consider the real function of these as a kind of compensation for the lack of contact and warmth. Warmth, tenderness, security, etc, cannot be bought with money or objects. This partly explains the feelings for animals. One's own pet, or the dream of owning one, can fill one's leisure and the emotional vacuum—which exists, despite children's rooms packed with consumer goods and pocket money.

Parents more positive?

Parents, too, are generally content with their children's economic standard. Ninety-five per cent of 11-year-olds' parents and 90 per cent of 16-year-olds' parents thought that their children had enough money at their disposal. But in certain cases, above all in social group 3, the parents thought that their children has too little money to get by on. This was asserted by as many as 20 per cent of parents in social group 3, as against only 4 per cent in social group 1. Single mothers said twice as often as co-habiting/married parents that adolescents have too little money (22 per cent and 11 per cent respectively). These figures apply above all to the 16-year-olds' parents. The 11-year-olds' parents did not consider quite so often that their children had too little money to spend.

There seems, therefore, to be a feeling that the parents, especially single parents and those from social group 3, are more positively inclined towards consumption than the children themselves. There are many ways of interpreting these results. The parents in social group 3, had perhaps experienced difficulties in not having enough money when they were 15 or 16, and therefore do not want their son or daughter to go without, as they themselves had to. And of course teenagers' expenses are not felt so acutely if you have a high income. The finances of many working-class homes have difficulty in coping with the demands made by 16-year-olds, even if the parents think they are justified. It is also more usual for parents on a tight budget, single parents for instance, to say that they themselves have to give something up, so that their children can buy the consumer goods they want and need.

Judging by our study, opposition among today's parents against fashion is not very strong. Many parents consider *commercialism* or *fashion hysteria* quite a small problem compared with other, more social problems, such as, for instance, alcohol or drug abuse. Asked what would be the worst thing that could happen to their children, a very large group answered addiction to drugs or spirits. It is probable that parents do not spend much energy on training their children to be discerning consumers when they are most afraid of such manifest problems as drug abuse. Some of them perhaps even see buying clothes, etc, as a means of keeping the children away from social problems. When it comes to other leisure activities, such as supporting the children's hobbies, sports etc, we have the feeling that these motives are common. We believe that many parents accept fashion and consumption because they are glad that their children have an interest. It would be worse if they were not interested in anything at all—this is, no doubt, how many parents see it.

Commercial youth culture

The market's interest in children and adolescents is one result of the market revolution. Industry flourished and new markets were needed so that new products could be sold and the wheels kept turning. Children's and adolescents' leisure and culture have proved one of the new gold mines. In the 1950s the so-called *teenage market* emerged, reaching its zenith in the heydays of the 1960s. In the 1970s, it had become a multi-million industry throughout the world.[23]

Many youth cultures emerge as a revolt created by the adolescents themselves, in protest against the dominant cultures in society.[24] There were heated discussions about these sub-cultures in the 1950s, 60s and 70s. Mods, hippies and most recently punks. But the market is not slow to steer these protests so that they suit its aims. The revolt having been made fashionable, little remains of the original protest. The market also creates its own life-styles, which are continually made to change, at an accelerating rate. Variations in fashion are an example of that. Other expressions of culture, which are of importance to young people—films, dancing, music—are also exploited. This culture is an artificially contrived culture, as distinct from the culture which adolescents themselves create in their everyday lives.[25]

Commercialism—a concept of the times

Gradually *criticism of this commercialisation* of young people's lives begins to grow. Many have tried to define the concept *commercialism*. We can perhaps agree that it means a market whose goods and services are bought and sold for profit. But trying to define the concept is not particularly interesting. It is more important to try to illustrate how it has arisen and what it has come to represent. Historically speaking, it is new. It has been used to indicate certain weaknesses in the market economy system without one having to enter into discussions on the market economy as such. It has, above all, come to indicate what we in general disapprove of and fear within the market economy, the striving for maximum profit at any price—perversion, violence as entertainment, pornography, sexual prejudices, etc.

Commercialism also illustrates the *disquiet and fear* which parents, teachers and youth leaders feel, at the market's ability to captivate, i.e. commercial youth culture's attractiveness and the fascination that both children and adults feel towards much of what is offered by the mass market. At the same time we realise that these products, with their content, their form and the way in which they are put across, represent quite definite values. The market indoctrinates children, just at the time when many adults have renounced their influence. There is a strong reaction when many discover that the freedom from influence, which for some time formed an ideal among many adults, has been stolen by the market's producers. Never for a moment did the market forget the importance of influence and, then, often with values completely at odds with those which parents and associations want to convey. What we have stated shows, therefore, that it is not possible to limit or try to define this historically new concept and to understand its emotional content without having the socio-historical background clear in one's mind.

The market indoctrinates its children

It is almost pointless to try to define the effects of the artificial youth culture, what a particular cultural event, a particular film, etc, means to the public. One cannot trace certain events or products to certain behaviour in the individual. This does not preclude the ability of even an individual product having certain direct effects, but these are difficult to prove. Instead, it is more fruitful to try to discuss the more long-term effects. One theme that is beginning to crystallise as the most central is the *formational role* played by commercial youth culture.[26]

Commercial youth culture has assumed an increasing significance in training children and adolescents. The preconditions for this are shown in the above description of how the rural child becomes the market child, i.e. how changes in society have affected other important methods of cultural transmission, the family, other adults, popular movements, school. These influences are all, more or less, strong today.[27] In modern society, the educational process has grown more anonymous. Children and adolescents are left more to their own devices than previously. Peer groups have acquired ever increasing significance in social control and attitudes to symbols and values. We have described these changes earlier in the book.

Alongside this development, commercial youth culture has become an ever increasing source of values. Several conditions must prevail if this culture is to work as a formational force in society. The principal training of young people must take place within their own peer group, and parents and other adults must have abandoned, more or less, their attempts at influence. In this way the culture industry's products affect every single individual, not so much *directly*, as *by way of* the peer group. The effects of this indirect influence have greatly increased with the extension of childhood and adolescence.

Increasingly, it is the peer group which has come to help an adolescent to choose and, to some extent, also interpret the symbols and values with which he associates himself. The sources may vary, but without doubt one of the most important is the market's youth products. Parents and other adults accept, to an ever increasing degree, the values created for and by adolescents. We may even speak of *inverted socialisation* which gives the market even greater economic scope for its products. In practice it means that parents and other adults more or less accept that adolescents and commercial youth culture have taken over the doctrinal role themselves. It even seems that many parents are themselves being indoctrinated by the adolescents.

The market can often establish success if its products can reach the *pioneer* adolescents, those who have high status and a leadership quality, and whom it is important and attractive to identify oneself with and to imitate. The manufacturers and marketers also try to produce their own pioneer adolescents or 'in groups'. Idols are one example; another is when 'ordinary' adolescents are selected and equipped with the products that are to be sold and then used in a marketing campaign. We have seen how adolescents were first trained in skate-boarding and roller-skating and were then seen on the street scene as part of the marketing of these products.[28]

Commercial youth culture does not govern by force or formal rules. It usually operates with more sophistication than that, leading and indoctrinating the broad front of youth groups into its way of thinking.[29] It is assisted by packaging and form and 'the message', as well as by the values inherent in the contents. Sometimes the message is clear and easy to understand, but it is often concealed. Sometimes it operates only at the subconscious level. Our reports in the series *Till varje pris,* (At any price), show which themes recur frequently in the products of commercial youth culture; for instance, sexual prejudices, sex and eroticism, violence, fear and excitement. Another common theme is 'beneficial leisure', a time for self-realisation. Commercial youth culture continually prescribes consumption as an antidote to the difficulties of everyday life.[30]

The commercial magnet— attraction and fascination

Commercial youth culture is the market's gift to children.[31] Its dominance and attraction must be seen against the background of the living conditions which characterise or threaten children and adolescents in our society. For those having a clear picture of this background—the lack of responsibility, role and function, the vacuum, the lack of faith in the future, the passive role—it is not difficult to understand the attractiveness of what the market has to offer. In that sense we could say that the market guides and controls its children by consent. There is a conformity between the children's situation and needs, and the market's products and marketing methods. The market fills the vacuum and recognises the children's needs. In gives children a role and a function, and it creates an artificial participation, in exchange for the participation denied to children in the rest of everday life. The role of consumer is at least a role.

It's funny, before, when I didn't have a job and got 40 kronor a week, I was satisfied with that. Now if I sometimes have earned a bit less one week I feel quite lost, have no money to manage on. I nearly get into a panic when I notice that my money is nearly gone. Then I realise how grown-ups must feel, who have lots of bills to pay and that sort of thing.

Pia, aged 14

Children and adolescents, like adults, are searching for a purpose in life. It is not so easy to find models and identification in the adult world. In the absence of idols in everyday life, the idols in films, music, etc, play an even more important role. But this identification is often idealised. One problem is the general view among parents that children and adolescents should not be influenced. Children should be free to choose their own life-style and their own ideals. This has resulted in confusion and has made the search for a purpose more difficult; this is where commercial youth culture has stepped in. It continually produces values and chances of identification for children who are thirsting for purpose, responsibility and significance.

Commercial youth culture thus addresses itself to very important aspects of the children's and adolescents' existence. An important part of the producers' operational method is to try to get the children and adolescents to satisfy their needs through consumption. But this also means that commercial youth culture meets important needs in the children—needs not otherwise met in daily life, in the family, in school or in leisure.

The artificial period of adolescence, segregated childhood and youth from production and work, the hiatus between adolescence and adult life, the new special characteristics attributed to adolescents, the creation of a youth culture—all this suits the market which is not slow to latch on to young people's reaction to social and cultural changes.

The analysis of altered conditions in childhood has given us valuable clues to an understanding of the dominance and attractiveness of commercial youth culture. We can also seek an explanation of that attractiveness in the content and message which commercial youth culture puts over. At the same time, however, contacts with adolescents reveal that they often realise that the commercial products are bad and contain an unreasonable amount of violence-worship and sexual prejudice, and that people are influenced by advertising and commercial values. But this does not prevent the majority of adolescents, and adults, from being attracted to the market's products. Adolescents can often analyse why the cultural industry's products contain doubtful values; they *see* the deceit, they *know*, but that still does not prevent them from participating in what commercial culture has to offer.

Most of us probably feel drawn to things and events from which, in principle, we would prefer to keep our distance. Adults tend to feel uneasy about the content of the commercial goods, its message and doctrine, without understanding this *exploited subconsciousness*. There is also a risk that we will moralise about the participation of young people. When we concentrate on criticising ideology, i.e. are content to point the finger at sexual prejudices in weekly magazines, racial prejudices in comics, a worship of violence in films, and then leave it at that, we are doing no more than disclosing what most people, including adolescents, already know. At its worst the criticism of commercial youth culture becomes a criticism of its consumers.

We shall therefore try to illustrate further its appeal and its attraction, by analysing how it is related to important psychological facets of our personality, not always associated with the critical control of the conscious mind, but rather with the governing of our actions by our emotions and experiences.

Our need of fantasy

Fantasy, excitement, emotional experiences are important factors in child development. Fantasy is a creative force[32] which can make us imagine which results can be offered by different solutions to a problem. It allows us to imagine what society could be like. Its force provides hope. Fantasy accounts for an important part of culture's evaluating and reviewing role. It helps us to appraise our experiences. It can moreover be seen as the result of suppression—the means of flight in a difficult psychological or social situation or in the face of severe social pressure. Fantasy is connected with our ability to imagine something that does not exist. It is common in children's games which always take place in a more or less make-believe universe and extend far beyond the real situation. With the help of fantasy, children practise mastering reality.

Fantasy ought to occupy a high place in our society but children's fantasy is disciplined from an early age. In school emphasis is more often placed on adapting to reality and conveying scientific facts and information. Fantasy is given little scope. Modern parents and youth organisations have also often rejected fantasy in favour of descriptions of reality. But there is magic in the child's mind. For an 8-year-old the sun is alive, because it gives light and gives light because it wants to. A stone is alive because it will move, rolls down a slope. The stream is alive and has a will of its own because the water flows. No other explanation would convince the child. It is often pointless, therefore, to give a child scientific explanations until it reaches a stage of development at which it can accept these 'truths'. What is more, we often do not consider how easily we can suppress the child's important fantasising. A child's experience of the world must remain subjective until it can understand abstract concepts. But if the imagination is not given an outlet in everyday life it must find one at other times and in other contexts which will not discipline but will recognise the need for fantasy.[33]

Stories and myths

If we refer to developmental psychology we can explain the importance of fantasy for the child's understanding of reality. Many childhood experiences are needed to help the child find a purpose in life. During the course of its development the child must, step by step, discover its own ego. It learns simultaneously to understand other people better and can finally reach an understanding of that which is beneficial and meaningful for all parties, and can discover the boundaries that are so important in life. To find this deeper meaning in life, it is necessary to be able to cross the narrow boundaries of a self-centred life and to believe that one has a valuable contribution to make to life, both now and in future. Here fantasy is invaluable. It can sort out emotions, counter the fears and expectations which children have, and give acknowledgement to their inner problems.

To realise this, children need help in symbolic form to help them work through their problems. In all ages, tales, myths, oral and written stories have helped them to understand. More recent anaylsis has shown that the old folktales could meet most of the child's need for fantasy. They do not provide ready solutions but nevertheless indicate a way out of the problems the child is struggling with. They do not back away from many of the deep psychological conflicts which are part of growing up. They allow the child to imagine how it can utilise what the tale reveals about life and human nature. As the tale unfolds it coincides with the child's way of thinking and of experiencing the world.

Folktales helped children to sort out emotions and conflicts on a sub-conscious level too.[34] They systematically work on the child's subconscious problems. By identifying itself with the hero in the story the child could enter into its most secret conflicts, go over them, overcome the suppression and thereby get to grips with reality.

Throughout history, these oral, and then written, literary traditions have collected a great deal of knowledge of how people and, in particular, children function mentally, and have helped them to develop and come through crises.

Children have come to grips with the inner problems associated with growing up, they free themselves from the child's dependence and gain self-reliance, self-esteem and moral responsibility. The child must therefore be able to translate what is happening in the unconscious to the conscious plane. When the unconscious ego is suppressed it ends up by being partly overpowered by unresolved conflicts from the unconscious. The individual may also have to

exercise such strict self-control that it can lead to mental problems. But if a certain amount of material from the unconscious is released to the conscious and is dealt with by the imagination, it loses to a large extent its ability to harm ourselves and others.

Many people think that children should be protected from their conflicts, their dread, their confusing, angry and violent fantasies, and instead should come into contact only with realities, pleasant fantasies and nice stories, but there is really no reason to keep from children the fact that all people, themselves included, have the tendency to act violently, asocially, selfishly, in anger and with *angst*. Children know that they are not always good themselves. It is just stupid to deny it. But they need symbolic descriptions of how best to tackle these problems.

When we abandoned fantasy and the folk tale we forgot their attraction and significance for our psychical development. But the 'experience industry' has not made that same mistake. It is prepared to exploit fantasy and to channel it in its own tracks. The culture industry has taken an almost irrecoverable lead today, when it comes to the control of fantasy products. It has a monopoly on dreams, myths, sensuousness, vehemence and excitement. It produces new heroes, witches and trolls in film after film, in children's comic after children's comic.

Folk tales have vanished in today's society. Myths and magic have been declared dead. Not even religion, which also deals with people's *angst,* has survived this departure from myths and belief. But the conflicts remain. Where can children and adults, with the help of fantasy, sort out their inner conflicts today? It should not be too surprising a fact that commercial culture supplies such material. It binds us even more firmly to the market.

Emotions and experiences

Psychology often distinguishes between a pleasure-seeking ego and a rational ego, which belong to different stages of our development. The pleasure-seeking ego belongs to our unconscious instincts whilst the rational ego is part of our conscious mind. It is among other things the conflicts between these two egos which traditional folktales work upon. Inhibitions within one or other of the two areas create desires which the individual is not allowed to indulge completely. This, in its turn, creates miscalculations. Instead of real satisfaction, fantasy moves in. Fantasy is always able to seek out pleasurable paths not inhibited by social demands; but it can also give the idea that things missing in the individual, or which he is cut off from, are of more value than they really are. If I feel harassed by the demands made upon me, I can dream about some idyllic place or look back on a happy event. And if I forget where the dream arose, I can perhaps believe that the dream is reality. This is neither realistic nor logical in relation to reality, but it is logical in relation to the wishes, miscalculations and conflicts. The pleasure-seeking at which the culture industry's products are aimed, and the form or packaging in which they are conveyed, often goes back to stages in the individual's development where the conscious mind could not cope and could not correct, except where what we would call a *childish omnipotence* reigns.

The individual constantly seeks to return to balanced instincts. It is this, among other things, that he/she is searching for in the products of the entertainment industry, which is not slow to supply the demand. Here the desire principle is given almost sole dominance. We have to fall back to a stage where we react with our *emotions,* not our minds.

The fascination we feel, for instance, towards an advertisement, can re-establish childhood desires and idyllic emotionalism. That is why it is so important to understand the emotional reaction to experience created by the culture industry.

Rhythm is another central aspect of this aesthetic fascination—it becomes important to find a way of re-establishing man's basic rhythms, the rhythms of breathing, of heart-beat, and of sexuality. One often finds this basic human rhythm in mass culture. It has immediate and instinctive human appeal. The attraction has to be understood emotionally instead of rationally. A lot of the pulp literature and popular music, such as disco music, contains such human rhythms. It offers an emotional experience and nothing one can, or even trouble to, understand. Against this background we can see why techniques for engaging emotions and experiences become more and more important for commercial youth culture. This is where research funds are being invested. Sales successes are assured if technique, colours, sounds, movements, rhythms and desires have their effect on the recipient.

The attraction and fascination have thus to be understood, in the first instance, in terms of experiences and emotions conjured up in the recipient. These emotions often have nothing to do with our conscious ideology. Ideologically, we may well keep aloof from some goods, but our emotions are attracted all the same. It is not just our thoughts, our conscious mind that dictates our actions but to a large extent the body, the feelings, the unconscious.

Fantasy and identification

Fantasy is also of great significance to identification, which is an essential part in forming the individual. In a normal case, society and adults afford the opportunities for positive identification, which strengthens the ego more and more. The less well this process functions—if there are not people to identify oneself with, or if adults do not help the child—the worse the individual's self-awareness becomes and the easier the identification with the products of mass culture. The changes in society that lead to a weakening of the ego, to unrealistic ideas of one's own ability, fear of deep emotional contacts, make it extremely important to find a substitute identification. Adolescents look for it within their group of friends and/or in commercial youth culture.

For an individual with a weak ego, identification is immediate and swift. Many adolescents identify themselves by quickly changing their models, without going through any real identification. Something that is easy to identify oneself with, or easy to plagiarise, is also attractive. Identification that requires preparation or reflection is less so. Life becomes constantly transient, while commercial youth culture, which, in an ever accelerating tempo, has specialised in selling continually new life-styles, makes new conquests. Life-styles and ideals become throw-away articles, just like consumer goods.

The manufacturers of commercial youth culture are aware of our psychological profiles and problems. Knowledge of psychology is used to make goods as attractive as possible. Experience or their researchers tell them that people's mental reaction is most often emotional, rather than rational. We all have our inner needs, dreams and unresolved conflicts. They may concern companionship, affection, etc. It is above all our unfulfilled and unresolved needs and desires which the entertainment industry latches on to. By looking at ourselves and our own needs, dreams and desires, we can understand the pull that the commercial culture exerts. Its merchandise appeals to the conflicts inherent in most people from various generations. This pull is influenced by the social conditions we live in. Needs change and every generation has its tender spots.[36]

Mass culture also expresses customs, desires, apprehensions and requirements at different stages in society. The culture of the mass media has to strike something that is essential to us if it is to succeed. The popular literature of today has new features. James Bond's world is not just a world full of inner conflicts but rather a world full of gadgets—its excess of technical elements is a sign of that. Bond's relation to the world around him is a material one. The structural background is such that it has become increasingly important to find outlets for goods on the home market. The customers' requirements have to be stimulated to increase the market's sale of consumer goods. To achieve this the market has developed a world of pretence, a world full of promises—a *material-aesthetic world*. Objects must be made attractive.

This industry of experiences and consciousness overwhelms young people with its products including the electronic sensuousness and vehement emotions of video and sound recordings. They encroach upon the formation of ideals and values. They channel protest and pretend to be a counterweight to society's calculating logic. With effective production and marketing methods, they appeal to the young consumer's irrationality and idleness. Their commercial powers develop ever better planned marketing projects, directed at an increasing number of target groups. The market is supported by a quick turnover of goods. The utility value of the products decreases. The system encourages waste of economic and human resources. Thus commercialism's 'negative effects' deal not just with youth leisure, but have long-term consequences for young people's future and for the kind of society and view of humanity they will take over.

Selling to the child of the market

Advertising has a turnover of some six billion kronor in Sweden. It is often criticised for forcing itself on the individual, for being emotional, giving a false picture of reality, arousing discontent and creating needs. In recent decades marketing experts have learnt how to use psychological knowledge to their advantage. Our innermost weaknesses and needs are exploited systematically. Both the conscious and the unconscious sides of our mind are assailed. This development has made a lot of advertising dishonourable and harmful to society.[37]

Our own studies show, among other things, how the producers employ so-called *hidden* and *total marketing*.[38] Hidden advertising should not look like advertising. Articles are smuggled into advertisements about quite separate items or are planted on hired people in town. Total marketing employs simultaneously a great number of different channels to get across its sales message. Films sell jeans and jeans sell films, etc.

Advertising does not necessarily have to be negative. Companies must be able to inform potential customers about their goods. But it should not be unreasonable to demand that advertising be truthful, i.e. factual, and that it should describe the actual qualities of the merchandise, both good and bad. A positive advertisement should, moreover, be independent of the customer's values, conceptions, reactions and weaknesses.

A sales message, for instance, which claims authority, does not belong to factual advertising, but study after study shows that most advertisements contravene most moral rules. In general, they aim at influencing and changing the consumers' values. The point of departure for marketing is, most frequently, not the physical qualities of the goods, but the customer's qualities and weaknesses. Knowledge about consumers is exploited in adapting marketing

73

strategy so that it 'hits home best' among them. Marketing is adapted to certain needs or values that the consumer is assumed to have. It conveys false assertions, or assertions that give a false impression of the product's properties. Very often the sales message gives incomplete information. Uncomfortable facts are kept back, etc. Often the advertisements encourage impulsive action. They try to get the consumer to act without thinking, subconsciously, automatically, impulsively. It may be a question of arousing emotions and conscious or subconscious sexual instincts. By these means, they try to make it difficult for the consumer to make an independent choice.

Emotional, unfactual 'life-style advertising' obviates the very free choice which the market economy cherishes. Even if we learn to be critical and see through the advertisement's message, we very often cannot defend ourselves against its influence. We are most vulnerable to the advertising that influences us at the subconscious level.

In 1957, Vance Packard was already criticising advertising for exploiting psychological knowledge to achieve its aims.[39] In *The Hidden Persuaders* he described the enormous investment advertising companies made and are making in psychological research. They tried to ascertain why consumers react in certain ways, and how to persuade the consumer to buy one's own particular brand, by increasing knowledge of the consumer's conscious and subconscious needs and motives. Thus they wanted not only to learn how people function, but also to discover their weak spots, which may then be exploited in marketing strategy. A series of experiments were carried out using more and more planned psychological methods. Today, for instance, there are methods of so-called subliminal influence, i.e. an influence below the level of consciousness.[40] Pictures and sales messages that cannot be perceived by the conscious mind are integrated into advertisements and are registered by the unconscious mind. The arrival of psychology in marketing changes its direction completely. By means of the new advertising methods, one should:

☐ Sell emotions to people 'poor' in emotions
☐ Sell reassurances of worth to people who felt worthless
☐ Sell ego-gratification to those with a weak ego

74

- [ ] Sell a creative outlet to people who have no such outlet in their daily lives
- [ ] Sell love objects to people who have not experienced love and affection
- [ ] Sell a sense of 'roots' to people who have broken away from their home
- [ ] Sell immortality to people afraid of their approaching death
- [ ] Sell sexuality to those who are sexually inexperienced.

Advertising aimed at children

Advertisements aimed directly at children and adolescents, not least in comic strips and other mass culture, are common. In addition, children are of course exposed to all the ordinary advertisements around us. A lot of it is 'nag advertising', i.e. its purpose is to make the child pressure its parents into buying some article or other. These goods are, in general, not bought by the children themselves but by their parents or other kind adults in their vicinity. Many advertisements concern what we could call child-capital-goods, i.e. quite expensive goods that the children have to acquire by nagging.[41]

Companies probably direct advertising at children for several reasons; partly to sell goods to the children themselves and to the children via their parents; partly to *train* the rising generation to be good consumers. Companies realise how important it is to get different trade marks established in children's minds, and to encourage their desire to buy, and their wish to solve everyday problems by consumption. Many advertisements sell only the actual trade mark.

There is a decided difference between the vulnerability of children and of adults. The causes are concerned with developmental psychology. Children live with fantasy figures in their everyday life and unlike adults cannot distinguish logically between fantasy and reality. Myths rich in fantasy are important for children's development. We have already touched on how this part

Just imagine, if whey-butter makes me big and strong like Stenmark.

of the children's world is being denied to them. In *animistic* thought (i.e. the belief that inanimate objects are also alive and have a soul), a stone, the sun, a teddy-bear all have life. If a teddy-bear says in the advertisements, that 'you must eat this or that, and buy this or that', he is a real person with authority. Authorities are important, especially those one can identify with and try to emulate. Björn Borg is considered an authority not just on tennis, but also when he gives his opinion on clothes, sweets or food. If Ingemar Stenmark's strength, according to the advertisement, comes from his eating whey-butter, then that is a fact. It is characteristic that while children can very well accept adults' reasoning that their teddy-bear and the sun are not alive, that it is perhaps not quite true that it was the whey-butter that made Ingemar strong, they 'know' that the logical and 'scientific' views are not true. Market strategists, for their part, are in collusion with the children and for instance bring teddy-bears to life in their advertisements. In that way the market strategists, or their advertising, are considered, even by the children, to be more 'on their side' than parents or school. Advertising recognises the child's way of looking at things and of relating to the world, to myths, to fantasy, to the unconscious.

The slightly older teenagers are also more exposed to advertising devices than adults. We have shown how adolescence is often dominated by emptiness, uselessness, how adolescents are looking for a role and responsibilities, and also that the teens are a period of natural uncertainty and a search for an indentity. The marketers exploit this to the full. They fill adolescence with a new role, that of consumer, and offer in their advertisements identification objects, e.g. idols.

Selling implication

In our report, *Ej till salu*, we gave an account of a study we made of the advertisements in *Vecko-Revyn* (*Weekly Review*). We wanted to interpret or decipher the advertisements directed at adolescents, to see which themes occur and which symbols and implications these advertisements utilise.[42] It is important to try to understand the advertisements' messages and symbols. There are countless techniques for capturing our interest and making us good consumers.[43]

All advertisements are designed to sell products to the consumers, but they often do not sell on the factual properties of the products, but rather by making the products mean something special to us. It is much easier to sell a product if you are successful in presenting it in such a form or give such qualities as are known to attract the consumer. Products are sold by being given new values, which are known to be attractive *symbols* for consumers.

Advertising translates conditions in the material world into a form which means something in human terms. Material objects are given a new value, a symbolic value, in the process. The important thing in advertisements is how they get us to desire what is being offered. This is where the symbols come in. What makes the products attractive is that the advertisements furnish them with a symbolic value which has been transferred, for example, from a person or object already possessing a certain value, to the product on sale. The market strategists exploit that value. There are whole systems of such value implications. The advertisements refer to these systems and use them as value-conveyers. This is the way the material is used, the values behind the choice, the knowledge of human desires and mental conflicts which are the market strategists' weapons in making us good consumers.

An advertisement shows, simultaneously, a picture of a diamond, and a pair of lovers. The text reads 'A diamond—when you know the flame will never die — a diamond is forever'. Here the diamond is sold through being linked to the symbol of eternal love. After seeing the advertisement, the stone comes to signify more than just a stone. It has suddenly acquired almost human features. It has become a symbol of love that lasts for ever. In this way, a diamond, through an advertisement, comes to signify love and constancy, and the symbol of love and constancy becomes a diamond, which makes it especially desirable.

People and things become interchangeable. There are examples of advertisements where the products have become human and even 'speak' — 'Say it with flowers,' 'Gold says it all'. On the other

EN DIAMANT -
NÄR MAN VET ATT LÅGAN ALDRIG SLOCKNAR.

EN DIAMANT ÄR FÖR EVIGT.

SVERIGES JUVELERARE OCH GULDSMEDSFÖRBUND

Diamantringen, som har diamanter på 0.28 ct, kostar ca. 3 050 kr (jan. 1980, priset kan förändras). Gå till din juvelerare för mer information och en gratis Diamantbroschyr

A diamond—when you know the flame will never die. A diamond is forever.

hand there are advertisements which make people indentify themselves with a product so strongly that they *become* the product. We
all feel the need to belong, to have a social 'place'. It can be
difficult to find this identity. Advertisements offer us an imagined
identity. It gives us the social purpose we strive for, but naturally
within the framework of commercialism's ideology—we are
allowed to become one of 'the Pepsi-people'.

One method commonly used is to link a person with the product
one wants to sell. This is done simply by putting the person and the
product side by side. The person symbolises special values and
qualities, e.g. strength, freshness, luxury, sensuality. By means of
the advertisements the person's symbolic value is thus transferred
to the product, just as in the diamond advertisement, and the
product one wants to sell *acquires* the same value as the person
depicted. The person and the product become indistinguishable in
terms of their values.

In Sweden, crispbread is linked with people who for us represent
certain values. The advertisement should have a certain effect even
in countries where the people in the picture are unknown. Just the
pictures of their faces project certain implications. But the
knowledge of who these people are, what values Björn Borg,
Ingemar Stenmark and Linda Haglund represent, gives the impression of Wasa crispbread quite different qualities — strength,
fitness, clean living, sensuality, winning. This is emphasised by the
text: 'Wasa rye bread gives you backbone.' Quite often the
advertiser uses people known to be beautiful. In effect, we are
dealing with a very élitist view of people.

Concepts, ideas, values, qualities and emotions are, through the
advertisements, consistently linked with certain products by being
transferred from a person or an object to those products. Even if
we do not actually *see* the connection, we nevertheless register it,
more or less unconsciously; gradually we think that this new
significance existed in the product right from the outset. In these
ways product and emotion fuse together and function in the same
way when we make purchases, when we consciously or unconsciously remember the product's *new* significance. The product
becomes more pleasant and easy to sell.

The advertisements arouse feelings in us, but do not give direct
satisfaction; they promise instead that we shall achieve satisfaction

and pleasure, once we have bought the product. Through the advertisements the more inaccessible emotions and states of mind—love, wealth, happiness, etc—are linked with something accessible, i.e. the product. Advertising exploits emotions which are known to be important to the consumers. It sparks off the idea that emotions can be attained by buying the advertised product.

Once the product has been provided with an emotional value, we can then invert the whole thing and use the product as a conveyer of emotions. It then comes to represent a certain feeling. It may promise that a certain feeling will arise once the product has been purchased. 'Things happen after a Badedas bath.' The advertisement then shows that the product can *create* a feeling of happiness, excitement, love, sexuality. Finally, the product *becomes* the emotion, a *surrogate* for love, happiness, excitement.

If the product can *create* emotions or *become* an emotion, it becomes more than just a symbol—it actually becomes one with the emotion. If Pepsi opens the door to love, which, as we know, one is aiming at, the product becomes a kind of currency with which one can buy love and happiness. It furnishes a kind of intermediate currency between real money and an emotion. 'Money can't buy you love' — Pepsi can, and you can buy Pepsi for money.

The advertisements address themselves to us directly, converse with us; they appeal to us and encourage us to act. 'You there, you know who Björn Borg is, how significant he is, what you feel for him, what emotions he represents, feelings I daresay you yourself would like to have and share. Now, this product happens to have exactly the same values and qualities as Björn Borg. Wouldn't it be worth a copper or two to be able to share those feelings?' One picture says more than a thousand words. In an advertisement all those words are not necessary.

The need to be special, to have one's own value and to be an individual is exploited effectively in advertisements for adolescents. 'Jeans for individualists', that is to say, not for just anybody, not for the grey masses, nor for the collective, but for the *individualist*. The individualism offered by Mustang Jeans is symbolised effectively by the surrealistic picture of the young man, alone and free, suspended in the universe. Paradoxically, although the advertisement mentions individualism as a value, the manufacturer wants to sell as many jeans as possible, so that, if he is successful,

Jeansen för individualister

The jeans for individualists.

individualism becomes uniform. But we do not become individualists by looking at this advertisement. The idea is that the advertisement will make us feel as if we are individualists already.

Advertisements can tap many reference systems. People, objects and environments presumed to have a high value, become referees. Nature and things natural, science, magic, myths and sexuality are some of the most common. A manufactured product may seem unnatural. This can be remedied by placing it beside the raw material that was used (at best). The raw natural element now becomes a symbol for what culture, manufacture, has altered. The function of the raw object is to give the manufactured product a natural status, so that we can assign nature's quality to it.

Science is often used as a symbol in advertisements. Take for instance, the advertisements for acne treatments, where two pictures are shown, of a person's face before and after.

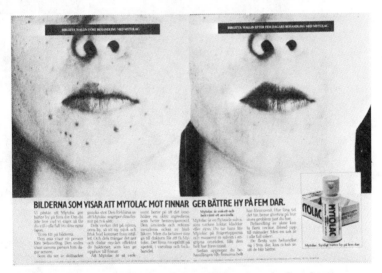

The pictures show that Mytolac clears spots in five days.

In our society there is a great need for myths and magic, as compensation for the belief in magic and religion of the old days. Here the changes are not given a scientific explanation, but rather the contrary—the explanation is magical and bewitching. Logic is

Wasabröc

Wasa crispbrea

er råg i ryggen!
Knäckebröd – det enda brödet som bakas på 100% fullkorn.

ves you backbone.

not of prime importance. The more incredible the results an advertisement can indicate, the more magic must have been involved. In these advertisements, it is the product itself which, in some magical way, produces certain effects. Things will simply happen in an enigmatic, exciting, magical but enticing way if we just buy or use the product. 'When a man you've never met before suddenly gives you flowers, don't be alarmed.' In some inexplicable way, you will receive flowers from somebody you do not even know when you are standing in the gramophone shop. Things which are incredible, but which many people still daydream about, happen in the world of advertisements. It will happen if I use Impulse (see illustration).

Lifeforce and resistance

What we have said so far about the child's role in our society, and its relationship with the market, perhaps gives the impression that most adolescents (and adults) have been completely swallowed up by the message of commercial culture and have wholly accepted its values. Such a view is misleading however. A dominant culture can never completely absorb subordinate groups. A certain resistance to cultural dominance always exists.[44] If we believe the contrary, we easily underestimate adolescents' ability to see through and resist the products with which they are inundated. At worst the adolescents appear stupid enough to dance to commercialism's tune and we close our eyes to the fact that they actually do get something essential out of this consumption too. There is a great risk of arrogance, if 'those who know better' stand aloof from popular music while adolescents listen, sing, and dance to it, because it immediately attracts needs not met in any other way. There is also a danger that a high-brow critic will merely play into the hands of commercial culture's marketing strategy. Even more people will be tempted to buy popular culture and turn their backs on the authorities and the kill-joys. The criticism can sometimes be just as good an advertisement as that put out by the companies themselves.

Flowers from a stranger—that's Impulse!

87

It is important to analyse the content of what we have called everyday culture, i.e. the culture that we ourselves create in co-operation with adolescents, or in co-operation between children and adults. We must not imagine that the commercial dominance has displaced other cultural patterns. What we take to be a complete acceptance of fashion trends and commercial life-styles may be superficial phenomena. We can also see adolescent sub-cultures as a protest or a revolt against the dominating culture and the underlying social changes; they are often a revolt against the obscuring and depoliticising of their lives. It is a collective way of trying to regain something of the social cohesion that has been lost.[45] It is above all during their leisure and as consumers of life-styles that adolescents can today find compensation and can work on the problems which are connected with the structural changes. These group cultures thus become a response to the dominant culture and sometimes also a direct protest against commercialised culture which is known to exploit them. Original punk rock is a good example of this. It grew out of basements and garages in working class districts, as a protest against unemployment and social rejection. But punk rock is also an example of how limited, as a rule, the effects of sectional culture protests are. There is a continual struggle between the dominant culture and sectional cultures, and one of the most devilish weapons the dominant culture can use is to accept the sectional culture. The commercial teenage industry has an enormous ability to incorporate and utilise oppositional symbols and turn revolt into fashion. The market thus tries to convert adolescent protest into a fashion and thus to disarm it. The commercial market also embraces its children's protests and revolts, and in this way draws them even closer to it.

We have at several points illustrated social changes, the consequences of which have evoked protests. The culture industry's products are often used as weapons in these protests. In attempts at protest, interest in pop music and idols plays an important part, in expressing otherwise forbidden emotions — sexuality, sensuousness, dreams of being someone, being someone else, about the right to be taken seriously. However, we must not forget the duality in this course — on the one hand, commercial influence and the incredible ability of commercial powers to utilise the need to protest;

and on the other, the use by adolescents of the culture industry's products in a kind of rebellion.

Adolescents do not accept unreservedly the ideology of commercial culture. They are not helpless objects or passive sacrificial lambs. An active choice is being made the whole time. Teenagers, and perhaps especially those who belong to a certain sub-culture, extract from the commercial life-styles, certain kinds of clothes, music etc, and adapt them to fit the key values in their own group identity. The varying life-styles are thus not completely absorbed, but on the contrary, adolescents have filtered, reinterpreted and adapted them. What we see of a sub-culture's style is a refashioning of different symbols from their normal social context, and of commercialised symbols into a new, complex whole with its own specific characteristics.[46]

In everyday culture, various groups with different resources are actively creating their own culture. This creative work is decided by many different factors: the chances of transmitting culture from generation to generation, of developing and creating self-confidence and identity, of fellowship and solidarity, class identity, awareness, etc. If this active construction of culture is to lead to essential changes, then the continued existence of its component parts must be assured.

Children have an enormous creative drive of their own, which helps them to withstand the forces trying to exploit them. In our conversations and interviews with children and adolescents, they expressed a robust life-force and awareness. Even those with a difficult upbringing and whose life is dominated by the mass media's values and life styles, show a great ability to resist and form their own ideas.

I can't go on my own to the council offices and say 'Why the hell are you putting up so much concrete?' They would only laugh at me. You've got to have a lot of people with you. It's the same with this Järvafält land they sold. They're going to build houses there now. It think that's wrong. There's nowhere you can go to enjoy the countryside. You've got to drive more than a hundred miles to get anywhere.

Bosse, aged 16

We have tried to explain which forces militate against individual creative work. Our analysis deals with both the grave structural problems in our society and the market's method of exploiting them. We have also tried to understand the attractions of commercial youth culture, how it fills a vacuum, plays on the child's need for fantasy, emotions and experiences.

The most challenging thing about our analysis is that society does not seem to want to avail itself of the child's unutilised awareness and resources, but seems, if anything, afraid of them. In the following chapter we shall discuss possible changes.

5   Our children and ourselves

Some starting points for change

The role of children in society has changed slowly, but throughout their history there runs a constant feeling of exploitation; from early industrialism's abuse of child labour to the abuse of children as consumers today. We can establish a clear link between the development of society, commercial dominance and conditions for child development. When the power of the market spreads, it creates the commercialisation of more and more areas of life. In this hunt for new groups of consumers, childhood and adolescence are brought into a system based on buying and selling. Social development which leads society into a useless period of waiting is a good thing for the market's purpose of achieving the largest possible profit. For the environment in which children have to grow up, and for their development, it is hard and demoralising.

The commercial market paved the way for social changes which in turn had a negative effect on the environments of childhood. Society as a whole became centralised while local environments, children's environments, became impoverished of social events. In the child's formative years, a vacuum was created, a feeling of uselessness, a de-politicising of social problems, lack of responsibilities, weakness of the ego and diminished faith in the future, the perspective of the onlooker rather than of the participant, where the ever present role of consumer should compensate for any deficiencies. Commercialism has gained more and more scope, the more useless children are declared.

The gap between ideals and reality hits children hard. The welfare state has officially proclaimed equality, fellowship, security, responsibility and development. But, each day, young people see a society where inequality is great and where human isolation is one of our most serious social problems. Those most vulnerable are those who live under difficult social conditions, those who cannot keep up with the competition, the handicapped, immigrant children. One way out of the conflict is drug abuse, another is vandalism, protest in both its acceptable and non-acceptable forms. Another solution is to devote great care to oneself and one's own personal development. It is easy to lose touch with the past and the belief in the future, and to live instead for the present moment. The commercial life-styles offer swift change. Even life itself is marked by the mentality of the 'throwaway society'.

How can changes be made? Are they even possible? And in what direction? What happens if we just sit on our hands? Where shall we begin? With production or reproduction? Production and the economy are obviously an important foundation for our society. We have pointed out weaknesses in the prevailing market economy system. As well as making us materially well off, this has created large and serious social costs and problems. The market promotes consumption as compensation for these deficiencies. The market's ideology forces out other ideologies. The market creates commercial exploitation and adversely affects conditions for child development. In the long term it is an absolute necessity to change the prevailing market economy, even if we must be aware of the difficulties of achieving any swift changes.

THE REALITIES OF EVERYDAY LIFE

Perhaps it is even more important to bring social reproduction into the political debate. It may be a relic from the patriarchal society which makes us stubbornly hang on to the idea that all changes in society have to start with production. This may be one of the reasons why social life has been forgotten, even in the most radical visions of how society should be changed.

It is important to discuss *everyday life*, the simple life which must be safeguarded and improved. The reality of everyday life, after all, constitutes the life and mainstay for young people too. This includes all the considerations of everyday life and how people organise the social life in the local community. People are linked with this reality, here and now, in the considerations of everyday life, and yet this sector of today's society is the most neglected and least noticed. Everyday life must be *seen*. That is where all great matters begin.[1]

CHOOSING OPTIMISM

Today's society has many different possibilities for development. It is difficult to predict which of these will dominate in the future. Many of today's problems give rise to a weakening of faith in the future, not least among young people. Our research indicates that most children and adolescents have a clouded view of the future. They do not believe in any positive social changes, but, nevertheless, do have a picture of what society could be like. Like them we too have a vision of how we can get ourselves out of the present deadlock. We have reached an important turning point—should we continue as before or work for a society based on the needs of its children? Change is, of course, possible, but it requires wholescale solutions and much revaluation of previously held truths. Great efforts from society will be necessary, the broad mass of the population must allow themselves to be committed to an optimistic future. Certainly it would be easier both for the authorities and for individual people to sit on their hands and wait for things to go wrong. But we cannot accept such a solution. Choosing optimism becomes a programme in itself,[2] even if we have to be aware that it is the most difficult path, and one which requires great strength, which makes great demands and which will assuredly be free of neither conflict nor problems.

Our divided economic system

In order to be able to discuss changes in everyday life, we take our economic system as our point of departure. Thus it obviously becomes important to seek changes in the divided system which we believe is firmly lodged in everyday life and in the *local community*. We can distinguish four divisions within the economic system—the *public system*, the *market system*, the *domestic system* and the *local* or *caring system*, as we call the system established in the local community.[3]

The *public system* is a political system with political aims. Its economy can be divided into many kinds of sectors and levels in the community—educational, cultural, and regional policy, also national, provincial and municipal levels.

The *market system* comprises many markets, in our society—the commodity, labour, capital and property markets. This economy is woven into the public system by laws and regulations of many kinds. For example, we have financial and taxation policy, economic, trade, labour market and environmental policy.

The *domestic system* comprises all private homes and households. This system is central to both the public economy and to the market economy. It provides basic care for children and adults and supports and facilitates all other enterprise within the market economy, as well as the public economy. The private household creates not only producers and consumers but also clients who require the services both of the market economy and of the public sector.

The *caring system* ought to comprise the collective activities based in some form or other upon common enterprise in a social network, in the activities of associations, in the protection and maintenance of the local environment etc. This system is more difficult to define than the others, and has seldom been the point of departure for surveys, research reports and political discussion. This economy is seldom accounted for in economic statistics, and yet surveys show that almost half of all work done in Sweden is within just this sector.[4] There are many reasons why this part of the total economy has difficulty in making itself felt in relation to other systems, and why it nevertheless is so valuable that it ought to be brought to light, strengthened and made noticeable. It ought to be able to solve many of the tasks of production which are concerned with the community and co-operation between children and adults at the local level. Furthermore it could form a base for nature conservation, deal with social renewal and caring, or production of goods and services in the form of common facilities.

There are three decisive reasons why changes corresponding to the above points of departure deal with renewing the caring system and its economy. Firstly, there is the question of establishing conditions conducive to a good upbringing for children and adolescents. Secondly, it concerns the discussion of the revitalisation of community life and how we organise our common affairs. Thirdly, we must find new ways of reducing the dominant influence of the market economy and of the commercial ideology over our lives.

Reasons for the caring economy

BETTER ENVIRONMENTS TO GROW UP IN

One of the chief reasons for our interest in the 'forgotten' community sector is that many young people are rejected by the market system, or have never been included in it at all.[5] They do not participate in paid work, since we have obtained a more and more exclusive labour market which does not consider or perceive that children and adolescents are an asset. Instead, children have to spend their time in a lengthy marking-time period in school and in leisure, waiting to become useful in production. They are 'declared useless'. This is a very happy situation for the forces which seek to fill the vacuum. The adolescents who, in spite of everything, have come out on to the labour market, are frequently more vulnerable than the adults. They fall victim to unemployment more often, and this unemployment hits them harder.

Only to a very limited extent do children and adolescents work together with adults. The gap and lack of contact which, these days, characterises the relationship between the generations is unsatisfactory for many reasons. There is increased pressure, meanwhile, on the public sector, which is supposed to provide means of support for adolescents or various forms of social work, such as schooling, etc. This need of resources is limited by increased requirements in all other areas, for example, social welfare, health care and the prison service. For the moment, the growth of the market economy which makes contributions to the public sector, has been slowed down; a consequence of this is, for example, further cutbacks within the public economy. This ensures even less scope for adolescents on the labour market.

Children have to feel useful, feel that they have a task and a role in society. It is a *fundamental right to be taken seriously*. Each human being has a need to feel respected as a special individual. We all have to feel that we are capable of something. This may be a question of practical and social skills or accomplishments, and has nothing to do with egoism but is an important part of the creation of the individual ego and of a social environment, which lets each person realise his own value. People seek a *raison d'être* and a role in society.[6] This is especially important in the teenage years, when one tries out one's own identity and searches for activities which give life fulfilment. We must understand the importance of children and adolescents being able to find this reason for living and that their assets are made use of. We all have *unexploited possibilities*. If we are not utilised in a meaningful way, then feelings of emptiness and insignificance arise. Being brought up in a good environment means, among other things, possibilities for taking responsibility and for participating together with adults. This is best attained by children and adolescents, together with adults, being responsible for common tasks, which are of use to the local community in which they live. Children have to be trained into their adult role. It is necessary that they should be able to learn from the experiences of adults. They have to learn independence, responsibility, equality, by practical use of these values in everyday life. In addition, it is important for children and adolescents, at an early stage, to gain positive experience of what work can mean, work as a cultural act, creative work. This provides social training and an awareness which is very important for the ability to influence their future work also.

The efficient market economy will, for a long time, probably be much too specialised for children and adolescents to be able to take part in production. The situation is just the same in places of work in the public sector. An investment in production within the caring sector would, however, give children and adolescents the opportunity of taking part in creative work.

Let us summarise what we mean by *good* environments to grow up in:

- [ ] environments which children can relate to, so that children can participate in community work

- [ ] environments where the generations *co-operate* on important questions. Children and adolescents must be given the opportunity of growing up into the adult world, in a continuous process, with support from adults

- [ ] environments which provide *productive tasks* for all. This increases people's involvement and combats institutional thinking, passivity and the rule of the expert. Children must be given meaningful tasks, a responsibility and be able to develop their innate resources

- [ ] environments which give children *participation* in community work. They shall build upon tasks and responsibilities in co-operation

- [ ] environments *which combat social rejection* and isolation, encourage positive social control, build upon solidarity and fellowship and which combat the need for society's control apparatus

- [ ] environments which fill adolescence with *a reason for existence,* that is, which give self-esteem, identity, belonging, co-operation and followship

- [ ] environments which create *alternatives* to the commercial leisure and culture industries

- [ ] environments where adults understand the complete scope of the term 'our children'. All adults must realise that they have a responsibility to provide the coming generation with the security and development which they need to be able to function in the local community.

Good childhood environments are therefore an important starting point for good social changes.[7] If one has other goals in mind, then one will naturally come to completely different social solutions. The goal of social planning being based on what is good for children and adolescents, makes very definite demands for reform and change on a number of different areas of society, although clearly with the weight on what we have called the caring sector.

We must now take the consequences of what we actually know about the needs of children. In any other case, we risk again falling into a worrying conflict between ideal aim and reality. It is necessary to strive for *broad social solutions.* This means, among other things, that measures or ideas within one area must be seen in the light of measures within other areas of society. It also means that the goal of what is best for children must be paramount for the whole of social planning and then, above all, in the planning of the local community. With such a view, it is not possible to plan measures within one area which conflict with the aims we set up for reforming conditions for children to grow up in. Such a view of the situation in its entirety must dictate changes within the caring sector.

Many reports and much research have already established the need for better conditions for child development. In spite of this, different criteria have formed the basis for social planning throughout the years. Above all, the demands of the market have been given priority. Among other things, this has meant that we have beautiful aims and ideals on a wide range of social issues, while reality is often something completely different.

ORGANISING EVERYDAY LIFE

One problem is that the caring economy has had to take second place to the market economy and the development of the public sector. Both the market revolution and the public sector revolution have diminished the opportunities for children and adolescents, as well as for the elderly and handicapped, to take part in some area of production and the economy. Instead they are supported by the work of others and by the social security system.

The affairs people have in common have, to a large extent, been taken over by institutions with employed staff. This is so within the schools, the social sector, the leisure sector, the cultural sector, etc. The 'invisible' caring work of women has been transformed into paid work. The voluntary cultural efforts of the popular movements have in many ways been made municipal. This development is both to the good and the bad. It has provided more paid employment opportunities and created a well developed social service and social security system; at the same time, this creates insufficient involvement and passivity in facing up to one's own difficulties and those of other people. It is important to halt this trend, without 'disarming' the social security system because of it. People ought to be able to take collective responsibility for common affairs in a completely different way from previously. Some caring work can, for example, be run as voluntary work done by everyone in the community, both men and women, children and the elderly. There are many tasks within the social, health, leisure and cultural areas which do not necessarily have to be run as paid employment, but which could be included in what we call caring work.

In addition, the relation brought about by taking decisions together leads, immediately, to social consequences. A collective decision-making and administrative process in social matters results in those who take part in the work being forced to involve themselves in questioning, to study the social context, to experience what it is like to convey and fight for their rights, etc. *We are approaching the democracy of involvement instead of the service democracy.*[8]

Social problems are most often politically social. It is therefore important that people become involved, in order to improve the social environment. The state take-over of public dealings usually gets in the way of this, since the causes are most often sought in the individual. Organising certain social caring tasks and certain elements of welfare in local communities can combat the negative aspects of professionalism and institutionalisation.

Social renewal

The historical context helps us put today's problems into perspective. Retrospection bears witness to the almost unbelievable social and material development which our society has gone through. Even so, it provides grounds for the criticism of our present society. Many important features, which ought to be part and parcel of our social and cultural life, have been lost in the transition, or have never been given the chance to develop. When we speak of this, it is easy to come to the incorrect conclusion that we are romanticising the old days. It is, however, not a question of a nostalgic return to better times—times which never existed—but rather to capture values which should not be allowed to be lost, and which must be developed and passed on to future generations.

A *social renewal*[9] has to contain both preservation and reformation. Daily life has to be repetitive so that people may recognise themselves and find continuity in their existence. On the other hand, society must constantly be reformed and improved. Life in society does not permit any absolute solutions. It is a continual process. Each new generation has to 'recapture democracy'. This means that each new generation has to defend and transmit valuable knowledge about social life from previous generations, and at the same time reappraise and improve the living conditions for their own generation and those of the next.

There is no given form or given pattern for this social renewal. On the other hand, there are necessary conditions or processes, in the sense that, if society ignores them, social life ceases to function.[10] These processes are connected both with the development of the individual and with the organisation of society. The fundamental basis of social renewal could be social life within the caring sector.

Entity or commodity

Apart from material needs, human beings need to belong to a social network, in which we show that we care for others. We need to give and receive care and affection, *to love*. Our individuality is a matter of innate potential and is the driving force towards development.

The opposite is the isolated person, a stranger both to himself, to others and to society. Existing also means being respected as a person. The most important characteristic of the essence of existence is activity, the productive use of human resources. But we live in a society geared towards possessions. Our relationship with the world around us is coloured by the desire to *have* and to *own*.[11]

In caring work it ought to be possible to acknowledge the essence of existence. This should also counteract a materially oriented society.

Co-operation and solidarity

In a society where collective forms of co-operation are in a mess, the care of children and the elderly can easily get left behind. Developments have led to more and more individual solutions to social problems. Individualism is strengthened by the market, which makes capital out of campaigning for individual self-realisation. But that undermines solidarity, co-operation and community feeling. Common solutions, however, break down loneliness, isolation and privatisation in everyday life. This also means that the individual ego can develop in the collective process. We gain strong personalities, which can co-operate and function in a social group. In community spirit is born the immunity which acts as a buffer to the onslaught of commercialism.[12]

A caring economy should entail more people taking part in caring work among children and the elderly, and ensure that security for the handicapped, the elderly, the infirm is increased, and that community work is organised collectively.

The inequality of everyday life

The resources of society are unevenly distributed between the 'haves' and the 'have-nots' and also between different geographical areas. Certain formative environments are rich in activities which stimulate and develop, while others are impoverished and lacking in social events. We must stand firm by the aim of an equal division of resources.[13]

The establishment of effective caring production could combat the inequality of everyday life.

CURBING THE MARKET

Sweden has a highly developed market economy. Its present expansion, which is based on large exports, rationalisation, effectivisation, a mobile workforce, etc, happens at the expense of society, increasing pressure on the public sector. Many non-essential goods are produced while, at the same time, many essential goods and services never come out on to the market. There is an inbuilt system whereby goods get worn out quickly and resources are wasted, so that the producers can renew goods at an accelerating pace.

Work and the value of work has been altered by the different stages of industrialism. As most industrial work has become easier, so the demands for greater efficiency have meant that it has lost much of its content and meaning, and has been relegated to mere supervision. All its deficiencies are meant to be compensated for in leisure time, but surveys show that those who have good jobs in general also make good use of their leisure, while those who have strenuous, stressful jobs also have passive leisure periods.

The market economy makes a priority of economic growth and profit, at whatever the cost. It creates economic pressure and commercial exploitation, which especially affects children and adolescents and those other weaker members of society. What should expand is social and psychological well-being, through people developing themselves and gaining greater personal satisfaction from their work and their everyday existence.

The market economy cannot be changed overnight. In the future, too, we must have close economic and cultural ties with the rest of the world.[14] We have to trade with other countries and are forced to maintain competitive industry. A large proportion of our production has to go in exports and we are required to import goods from abroad. A great amount of production for ourselves also has to be made in large-scale economically profitable units. In the future, too, we will be dependent on technical advances and development within industry.

A change in the market economy is a necessity in the long term. It ought not to be possible to prey upon nature and upon human resources. The forms of ownership are also problematic. An especially important question is the dominating influence of multi-national corporations over our economy and our cultural and economic dependence on them.

But making investments in what we call the caring economy could also influence the market economy. We have described how part of the market economy's demand for efficiency, rationalisation and growth results from an increased need for social provision within the public system, the increase being needed in order to combat and lessen the social problems created by the market economy. A functioning caring economy would mean a lot to our everyday lives and our social conditions. In the long term it may diminish social problems. The social cost stemming from deficient living conditions, loneliness, children's vulnerability, etc, should thereby also diminish. This means that pressure for further growth in the market economy can also become less. In addition, a caring economy means that the production of many essential requirements is taken from the market economy to the caring sector. This implies that the production in question will not end up within the same system of buying and selling which now characterises much of the production of goods and services. If people themselves take responsibility for production of certain goods and services, this, of course, would mean competition for the market economy and would so lessen the dominance of the market over our lives.

Awareness and the habit of critical thought are required in order to see through the commercial ideology or to be able to take any responsibility at all for its actions, and to be able to influence the development of society. Such awareness does not come of its own accord. Parents, organisations, schools and adults in close proximity can co-operate towards a greater awareness and critical attitude amongst both young people and adults. Today other forces are paramount, encouraging non-awareness and non-critical thought—a form of ideological teaching in itself. All too many adults let children and adolescents down as regards their educational responsibilities.

The most important form of awareness is created in common experiences—awareness that what is done within caring production is important both for myself and for others. Here there are also opportunities for all adults to take the role of instructor seriously.

The local community as base

The base for the caring economy is the *local community*. By local community or local environment we mean a relatively limited geographical area. This might be a residential area, a neighbourhood, a village or similar. In general we take the residential environment as a starting point, but it might also be a group of people, e.g. a work team, a group of school pupils, etc. A functioning environment, which children and adolescents can also relate to, get to know and participate in, consists of perhaps 400 to 600 people, a maximum of approx. 1000 people of mixed ages. Another way to quantify local environments would be to set a limit at 200 to 300 households. This is a guideline for the future when new housing schemes are built. In present-day housing areas we can obtain such changes, but it ought also to be pointed out that there often exist natural and geographical areas which contain both lower and higher numbers of households than those given above as a guide. When one is discussing the size of a local community, one must try to emulate such natural boundaries.[15]

Caring work—what is it?

Caring economy, caring work, caring production. Why these new contrived concepts? It may be opportune to find a comprehensive term for the sector which has to be strengthened. In itself *caring* is not a new concept, but a convenient one. It arouses positive associations. In the following, this term will be given a very wide bearing. It means *caring for people*, especially children and the elderly. But it is also a question of the *work* and the *production* which occurs in the local community. Caring production can be composed of both goods and services and of cultivation and creation. The term caring also covers *looking after, preserving, protecting* and *not wasting* human, cultural and material values. In practice this implies, for example, repairing instead of throwing away, renovating instead of letting things decay unnecessarily.[16]

The *caring economy* has an important foundation which separates it from other economic systems; it is founded, in the first instance, upon voluntary contributions, upon *giving* and *taking* instead of *buying* and *selling*.[17] The work carried out within this economy is, in the main, unpaid.

Caring work is *unpaid* voluntary work, which is not given a monetary value. On the other hand, it has an immeasurable human value. It differs therefore, from work carried out within the market economy and the public economy, which is mainly based on paid employment. Caring work can be done by children together with adults who have their main source of income within the public sector, or the market economy. But pensioners and others who are, today, excluded from work, but who, nevertheless, would like to take part, may also do so on the basis of their own terms, interests and opportunities.

Caring work in practice—some examples of possible changes

In this section we shall develop further the ways in which the caring economy might be organised in practical terms. We want to emphasise that it is hardly possible to describe any cut and dried visions of the future. The tangible content of any change must grow from those whom it most concerns. Here we shall, however, try to illustrate some possible changes and the reforms which these demand.

Caring production implies production of both goods and services.[18] Each local community has to take responsibility, in different ways, for common affairs. A number of tasks within various areas of society and within production may be managed by those who belong to the local community. Children and adolescents will have a set place. This may be a question, for example, of tasks within the school, of social service, health care, culture, leisure, care of the young and of the elderly. It may concern direct responsibility for running cultural centres, cafés and club-houses, sporting and recreation facilities, day nurseries, playgrounds, etc. The residents in local environments can take part in work within various existing institutions, in order to relieve and complement the existing salaried staff. People's involvement may, in the long run, help to decrease the need for institutions.

The local community can also involve itself in the production of goods. Many of the items used within the various local authority institutions and items necessary for the continued existence of the local community ought to be able to be produced there in small workshops and market gardens, run by different associations and co-operatives. Repairs and production requiring greater craftsmanship can be transferred to the local community. Places of work can act as an important gateway, for adolescents, into their future productive adult role. It will give the elderly opportunities to work for long or short periods, or on a part-time basis. Finally, the middle generations, those who, today, mainly carry out normal production, will gain the opportunity to co-operate in local community production, by having their basic work period shortened.

We shall, now, once again, touch upon the three levels which we described in the introduction to this chapter—the conditions for child development, everyday life, and the market—and see how caring work can be organised around these.

CONDITIONS FOR GROWING UP; SCHOOL IS LINKED TO THE LOCAL COMMUNITY

The role of children is central in caring work; even pre-school children can take part. Children need to *play,* to *learn*, and to *work*. These three activities ought to blend into each other. Children who carry out work, play as much as they work; an element of learning is also contained there. Throughout time, children have wanted to imitate the work of adults, in order to learn, and thereby gradually gained skills and responsibility. In this section, we shall concentrate our description on slightly older children, those who have started school, and shall see how they can be given important tasks which both instruct and develop, throughout the whole of their schooling.

The internal work of schools is generally fraught with problems; pupils have a markedly receptive role and a striking lack of responsibility and influence. They can seldom be involved in taking responsibility for their working environment. School is too theoretical and frequently isolated from the world outside. Pupils are strangers to the most basic activities within the community. School has no contact with the world it tries to prepare its pupils for; the pupils are divorced from working life and productivity. Family life, working life, school and different youth environments seem to be kept in more or less watertight compartments. At best pupils can learn skills which they may find a use for at some time in the future.

The school's aims are good, but they are not related to concrete reality.[19] The policy is that a school should come into closer contact with working life and co-operate with society outside school. Such aims become quite futile if one does not also ask which elements of working life are good for the pupils' development and which part of the community the school is to serve when it opens its doors to the outside world. Pupils can scarcely have much to learn from the work of present-day, large-scale, efficient, competitive industry. What good does it do the pupils to 'come out' into a local community where, socially speaking, nothing happens, where there are no adults during the daytime, and which lacks production or work in which children can take part? The environment children live in or the area around the school generally has no workshops, small shops or industries. The only adults, apart from parents, who

107

have contact with children, are those who have as their profession the training and care of children, such as nursery school teachers and recreational instructors, etc. But they hardly give a varied picture of adults and their occupations. One of the most important changes, therefore, ought to be giving school a place within a system where the caring economy is an important part of the local community. This would give all pupils a good chance of participating in formative work together with other adults.

The local community, if it is organised according to the principles of a good caring economy, can give pupils useful skills, and unite practice and theory in a meaningful way. This is well in agreement with recent Swedish school reform proposals and the present aims of the school. But ideas must also be realised.

The most important reason why the local community is so important, is that pupils can relate to it. Pupils can get to know both its assets and its problems. But these positive experiences for children are not possible if we continue to separate the school from the life of the community. The child's fundamental school environment ought instead to be its local environment and its co-existence with adults who work there. School as a community institution gives opportunities for development and a sense of purpose if it is based on such foundations. The local community has to be brought into the school and the school must be integrated with the community.[20]

Before the pupils are thrown into the competitive system of the big wide world, they must be given an image of alternative work and alternative production which is built on principles such as equal value, fellowship and responsibility. Pupils and teachers, together with parents and other adults in the children's surroundings must be given the opportunities to build up an environment with democratic qualities where everyone feels that they are needed and are taking part. But for the local community to function as a pedagogical resource, there have to be adults present, men and women, during the day time, carrying out productive work.

A vital local environment can contain many different types of activity. Normal places of work for production of goods and services, institutions for care of children and the elderly, cultural and leisure activities, cafés, restaurants, club and sports facilities, audio-visual centres, shops, etc. All of these enterprises should have two aims. Firstly they shall be useful to the area and give the inhabitants a sense of responsibility and a more vital environment. Secondly they shall be able to act as places of apprenticeship for the children and youth of the area. If both demands are fulfilled, the community ought to enter in and give economic support to these productive units. The enterprises will enter a contract, so to speak, with the community to be responsible for certain pedagogical tasks, and will receive in return for this a certain 'instructor grant'. Children and adolescents will be allowed to work in these centres to learn important things. The work, so far as possible, shall be done by the children and adolescents as a part of the school day under the supervision and guidance of adults, who are employed within these concerns, or adults who do their 'caring service' there. *The purpose is that children shall learn through participation.* In this way pupils at all levels will have part of their school work taken up with caring work.[21]

Responsibility for running the school—part of caring work too

School is supposed to prepare children for adult life which has both rights and obligations, among other things. Qualities which are bound together with responsibility must be practised and taught. Today's pupils get very little chance to do this in practice. School democracy should not just be an empty phrase, only valid for small details, but pupils must also be allowed to assist in the planning of the whole range of school activities and in its decision-making processes. One way of making this a reality would be to give pupils more responsibility for the running of the school and its budget. Each school class ought to have their own budget which pupils, teachers and other adult employees within the school should administer. These resources should be used, among other things, for repairs, decoration of premises, purchase of materials or of food. In this way pupils would be taught from an early age to take economic responsibility.

The development of the school environment has often been motivated by the factors of rationalisation and economy. The traditional school meals service has been taken away from many schools and replaced by microwave ovens, the food comes from a central kitchen and is served on disposable plates. That kind of development may be rationalised, efficient and perhaps, in the short term, economically worthwhile. But it does not require all that much consideration to understand that, pedagogically speaking, it is intolerable. The best way to train pupils in their obligations is for the pupils to take part in the day-to-day running of the school. Each school class ought to be able to prepare their own food, purchase goods, etc.

School meals facilities are also a good example of the fact that caring work should not be made a motive for one-sided cuts in expenditure and for rationalisation. Giving pupils responsibility for the running of the school does not mean that present catering staff (or janitor, cleaners, etc) can be dismissed. In that case the pedagogical work would become impossible. Present staff become even more important in this new situation, since they gain new and important educational duties. The staff will organise and guide the pupils in their work. Even if the pupils carry out the work, they still need guidance.[22]

In the pupils' caring work, we must therefore count both the pupils' work in caring for children and old people, or other productive work within the local community, and the work they carry out within the school in the preparation of food and the running of the school. The work must be given a measure of continuity. During certain periods, the individual pupil will be part of a group which is involved in the running of its own school. This period may last one term. During another term, the pupil will take part in the production of goods and services, which goes on in the local community's workshops, associations, co-operatives, allotments, etc. During other periods, he/she will participate in the care of children or the elderly, preventive health care, etc.

Since caring work is so important for the child's development, time must be set aside for it. As regards time, the pupil's caring work should take up the equivalent of *one day per week throughout the whole of his/her comprehensive schooling*.[23]

Home classrooms

Most schools today are too large, and many are not suited to the sort of tuition based in the local community and which should function in the way the curriculum advocates. One of the first mistakes in educational technology was the system, especially in the higher year-groups, of making pupils move to a different classroom for each subject and for each teaching period. Most tuition could take place in so-called *home classrooms*.[24] There are not many subjects which require special facilities. Some instruction could also be given outside in the local community, for example in other premises within a housing area, community centre or village hall, etc.

Each class should have its own home classroom for the whole of the comprehensive school period—a minimal demand in today's state of affairs. A home classroom is especially important for the lower year-groups. This would give pupils the chance to remain in the local community for as large a part of their schooldays as possible. In the long term, these could be situated outside in the local community. Each class would then get its own premises, a flat in a housing estate, for instance, or a villa, parts of a farm or in the old country schools which have been closed down. These premises would not only function as classrooms, children could prepare their meals there, too.

Co-operation between age-groups

It would also be an advantage to have greater co-operation between classes as there actually was, for example, in the B-school system (small rural schools). Older children are important for the young ones, when it comes to passing on skills, games, songs, etc. But we have often separated the small children from the older ones, for example, by having special schools for the different levels. This gives rise to important consequences in children's culture. Different age-groups must be included in the classes, especially if the home classroom is to be re-situated in the local community. One way might be to let pupils from the lower and middle school work in the

112

same classroom. Co-operation between the different levels is a good thing altogether without having to create larger classes because of it.

No contempt for skills

What we have said here about creating opportunities for pupils to co-operate in productive work does *not* mean an undervaluing of the need for skills at school.[25] Basic accomplishments such as reading, writing and arithmetic are obviously an absolute essential if, out in society, pupils are to be able to cope.

Pupils must realise that school is there so that they will learn, gain skills which will be useful in future life and which will affect their future employment. But much of the learning in schools is artificial and taken out of its natural context. Children see no sense in acquiring knowledge for its own sake. Formal tuition would also gain greater effect if it was based on natural practice, and the related social learning would be much more effective: it would seem relevant and fit in to its proper context. Words and terms for common experience of time, place, cause and effect, definitions of social values such as consideration and discipline gain relevance and can be used as a basis for work within different areas of knowledge, different departments and disciplines. Swedish, arithmetic, physics, chemistry, history, social studies, become aids for placing experiences in their proper context.

Caring work as training

We have highlighted the important role of adults as educators. Children and adolescents need to confront norms, values, skills, experiences, limits. Fear of having influence is damaging since it leaves the field open for ideological indoctrination by commercial forces. School as an institution naturally has an important part to play in training, but school should not take the sole and isolated responsibility for the training of children. It is not possible, as a

113

parent or other adult, to pass on all responsibility to the school. Education belongs just as much in the social life outside the school as in the school itself. Adolescents must also meet positive adults outside school, who can give support, make demands and have ideological influence. This could happen through the pupils participating in productive work and fellowship together with their parents and other adults in the local community.[26]

ORGANISING EVERYDAY LIFE

In this section we shall discuss the way in which some parts of everyday life can be organised as caring work.

Our analyses of the problems of caring and family in our society are disquieting. The crises of the welfare state are expressed in loneliness, isolation, rejection, a feeling of helplessness and alienation. We do not get the opportunity to involve ourselves in co-operation to solve these problems. People expect the responsibility for these solutions to be society's, and society has successively taken on more and more tasks in the social field, notably childcare and care of the elderly, the infirm and the handicapped. This trend has been necessary in a society which, in itself, harbours demands for security and solidarity. The swift movement of population has meant that the social structure has given way. The young and strong have moved away, placing even greater demands upon society's resources. Rejection in working life has become harsher. This, too, has placed greater demands upon society. An important element in the woman's struggle for equality is not just the right to work, but also the real opportunity to do it. This has entailed greater demands upon the community's childcare facilities, but these are far from adequate.

How can these problems best be solved in our time? Many wish to weaken the solidarity of the community. It is proposed that private interest should take over important parts of the public sector: people would once again have to pay for services received, and treatment and care would be run on a commercial basis. But this would mean the total collapse of the welfare state. Such a social attitude is naturally totally irreconcilable with the arguments which we have set forth here.[27]

But there is need for further discussion and reappraisal of many aspects of the present-day public social security system. The caring sector can function as a resource for the public system. *Everyone* should feel responsible. As an integral part of the collective sector people should have a right and an obligation to work with common everyday problems, outwith their salaried working hours. This may of course come to mean that there will be a redistribution between the public sector and the caring economy, and between the market economy and the caring economy but this will also mean that the economic resources within the public sector can be devoted, for example, to the health service, since resources will have been made available from other parts of the public sector. The combating of today's social rejection is a matter not only of human resources but also, in the long run of socio-economic profit.[28]

A vital, productive residential environment

One of the greatest problems is the lack of social activities in residential environments. The impoverished housing estates are not conducive to child development, since they are so devoid of social activity. Residential environments and local environments are closely linked to one another. Many people certainly think of the housing estate as their own local environment. Households in these areas often have many things in common which affect housing among other things. It is important therefore to try to re-create *productive housing environments*.[29] This would involve social renewal. In these productive environments, families and individuals could be included in a functioning social network, re-inforced by people using their own resources, in taking responsibility for collective affairs. Residents must, for example, be able to influence and constantly change the environment in which they live. The caring economy and caring production are our most effective means of developing this.

Workshops, light industries, local shops and restaurants are examples of productive activities in housing areas. Residents can also organise allotments and gardens, where crops can be grown for domestic use of for consumption within local authority institutions. The most important dimension is work and the production of necessities. Other examples are meeting halls owned by associations, cultural centres, small community centres, museums of local culture, libraries owned by associations, exhibitions, theatres, bookship cafés, cinemas, small shops, etc. The list could be long. Activities contribute to the creation of living areas, where a lot of things are going on, and thereby also create good environments for children to grow up in.

An amateur is a lover

A proportion of social care and service can be conducted within the local community. We have summarised service and caring as the activities which everyone aims at, to prevent people from falling out of the group. The activities are concentrated upon situations and conditions where the risk is greatest; for example, when we are small, old or infirm, when we are subject to psychological problems, drug abuse, etc. The point of this care is to keep the individual within the community. For this care to work, there must be a network of people who are willing to be involved. The measures we would take in this area are aimed at creating a medium for as many as possible to take part in caring work. We will be able to talk of an *amateurisation* of caring work. . . . Literally, amateur means '*one who loves*'.[30] The less efficiently this amateur caring work functions, the greater the amount of professional support required. Residents should themselves be able to organise part of what is today included in the public social services. Parents may work in child-care facilities where their children are placed, or in the schools, in order to relieve or complement the staff there. There ought also to be opportunities for adults without children, and for adolescents and the elderly, to participate in work within, for instance, the care of children and the elderly. For pupils from nearby schools, work in playschools, whether they be run by the local authority or by co-operatives, will become part of the work

which they carry out as their local community caring work. The system offers a number of advantages. Parents will have more time with their children and at the same time will be relieved of some of their parental caring duties by their children also being able to meet other adults in the local community. However, trained pedagogical staff must still be on hand, part of their duties being, among other things, to give guidance to the amateurs.

Even if more people can be involved in local community caring work, there will have to be institutions which have adequate numbers of trained staff. But it is possible to hand over some caring, social and preventive medical work to the residential areas. Many parents try, even today, to organise childcare themselves or together with other parents. Many are forced to do so, since there is a great shortage of places in day nurseries. Society ought to support and facilitate such initiatives.

A right and an obligation

Most people today are not involved in social work and caring. It may be easier to leave the problems to society and to the experts. But in a democratic welfare state everyone has both rights and obligations. It is not possible to shirk one's civic responsibilities by paying one's taxes. Most people—children, teenagers, adults and the elderly—could take on responsible tasks within social caring and service, tasks which in the long run may reduce the number and work of institutions. Everyone can come forward on their own terms and interests.

Mutual co-operation in residential areas gives natural opportunities for the nurturing and transmission of skills and experiences from generation to generation. It gives parents and also other adults better chances of involving themselves in the education of both their own and other people's children. This presses home the understanding that it is everyone's responsibility to be involved in caring, social aid and education. We cannot leave the educational role totally up to children's institutions or to the school, least of all can we accept that the commercial youth culture gains a monopoly on upbringing and influence. Responsibility is a duty, which everyone ought to recognise, since it is essential if the market's children are to become our children.[31]

Shorter working hours for all

The question of shorter working hours has been discussed for a great number of years. Many people have highlighted the necessity for parents of small children to have more time to spend with their children. It has also been maintained that a working day of six hours, for example, would compensate for longer journeys to work and would help to break the isolation of families. Many of the motives for shorter working hours are concerned with the desire for a better quality of life. But it is doubtful whether a system of shorter working hours which on its own would introduce more leisure time is really what we need just now. The most important reason for shorter working hours is rather that such a reform would almost be a prerequisite for the development of community caring work. The new free time arising from a decrease in working hours to six hours, could not be taken as *leisure*, but would have to be linked with caring work. Some form of community service is no new idea. Many others have touched upon this idea before. It is important for everyone to take part in caring work, including children and the elderly. The schools' involvement in this has been dealt with already. It would be beneficial to many old people if they were allowed to join in on their own terms and interests. They would provide invaluable experiences and knowledge. Finally, everyone who has their source of income within the market economy or within the public sector will have to play their part. For this group, a shortening of the working day will be essential if they are to have time and energy enough to participate.

Counteracting social rejection

Strong local communities, a school which seems meaningful, and caring work which provides role and responsibility, do not create such great social rejection as does the society of today. Among other things it entails another form of social control, which is founded upon most people knowing each other, working together and spending their free time together. Properly functioning social networks do not allow social rejection in the same way as when no-one takes any notice or shows concern. There is also economic gain for the community whose different institutions and authorities would not be occasioned such great expense for care and treatment.[32]

In the present situation an extra large caring investment is required to reintroduce rejected adolescent to a tolerable life. Our economic studies show that social rejection, for example in the form of drug abuse, entails great social cost. They also show that even the most expensive contributions to care and treatment are socio-economically worthwhile if rejected adolescents can be re-habilitated. Most expensive of all would be to do nothing.[33]

Social and mental problems also arise in communities with strong social networks and efficient caring work—problems which in different ways require care and treatment. But strong local environments can, in a different way from today, get involved in caring and remedial work. After a relatively short stay in an institution, many abusers would be able to join the local community circle and enter into employment, and in that way get the support and the control they require, to be able to refrain from further abuse.

Greater security for vulnerable groups

Many groups are especially at risk in our society, including immigrants and the handicapped. Many immigrant families face great problems when they come to Sweden. There is a great transition from the family culture and the living conditions of the native country. The children are often the ones most at risk. They easily get caught between the principles and culture of their parents and the ideology of the new society, of their friends and of commercial culture. It is clear that Swedish society has not shown enough consideration for the fact that Sweden is now a multicultural country.

A change in everyday environments would also give support to immigrant families. Their isolation could be broken by giving them responsibility for joint activities, just like other families. The act of having dealings with each other in everyday life, even in childhood, can bridge over some of the unnecessary gulfs which exist between immigrant children and Swedish children.

This would reduce prejudice and hostility to immigrants. It should also lessen the commercial pressure which many live with. Immigrant families could teach Swedish families a lot about family and relations, things which have been lost in western culture. Even today a lot of craftwork and other small-scale production is carried out by immigrants. We ought to take a lesson from that. Immigrant families often have a closer pattern of family ties than Swedes. In immigrant organisations it is, for example, almost unthinkable to arrange activities which are split up into age-groups, something which is so characteristic of a large part of Swedish social life.

On the other hand, some immigrant attitudes should not be thought desirable. Take one area where the cultural differences become quite tangible, the area of relationships between the sexes. Immigrant women are subordinate in a society which talks so fervently about equality. Their position has changed by moving to a new homeland.

In general the women had a more significant role in the farming household they left, even if that role was minor. In Swedish society, they have usually lost their productive duties and become even more subordinate to the men, who find employment, have Swedish lessons and make contact with other people. Through co-operation with Swedish women, immigrant women could learn a lot about the struggle of Swedish women for equality.

The handicapped are still vulnerable in a number of ways in our society. The high degree of efficiency in working life seems to leave no room for the handicapped, among whom unemployment is significantly higher than among non-handicapped people.

In caring production, there would be tasks for *everyone*, regardless of any reduced working capacity. Everyone should be able to enjoy carrying out useful work for the common good. The handicapped who, more than others, are dependent on a helping hand in certain situations, could feel more secure in a caring economy, while they themselves could have some significance in all the areas in which they are not handicapped. Instead of the

121

hundreds of thousands of kronor per year, which a place in an institution costs, collective resources could be used for integrating the handicapped into normal residential areas—always provided that a functioning social network exists which will lend its services.

Collective forms of living together

The family as an institution is not yet redundant. Strong and secure families are, among other things, an effective brake upon the commercialisation of our existence. It is the families who live in weak social situations who are also hardest hit by commercial pressures. The small, badly functioning family is especially vulnerable to commercial marketing. The vulnerability also lies in isolation and the lack of a functioning social network.

We ought to encourage more forms of collective living. These might be based on family ties, but other sorts of extended households also ought to be encouraged. Housing ought to be planned with consideration for the extended household's need for fellowship and mutual caring. Different forms of collective living and collective use of service facilities and household machines could be encouraged. In its extended form this would stimulate people to more joint consumption, mutual care, education and local production. An extended concept of the household could also have positive effects within cultural and immigrant policy, by its links with the traditions and requirements of many immigrant groups. We ought to appreciate better the skills and experiences which many immigrant families have in this area.[34]

CURBING THE MARKET

Why have we chosen to give prominence to the caring economy in the struggle against commercial culture? The most important reason is that caring work and activities run in the local community create concrete alternatives to the commercial leisure and culture markets. Local environments of a more vital, eventful and socially secure nature are created. The need to turn to commercial leisure environments will diminish. Within caring work there will be meaningful tasks for all children and adolescents, reducing the requirement for compensatory consumption to 'fill in time' or to 'make life fuller'. A caring economy could offer a number of concrete alternatives to the commercial facilities for entertainment and for meeting people. Children and adolescents, working together with adults, could run dances, restaurants, cafés and other entertainments themselves, without these being affected by commercial interests.

Leisure as work

In our society, leisure has increasingly come to play a compensatory role. Most children and adolescents live in a vacuum of leisure. A strategy based upon strengthening the caring sector in society emphasises voluntary community work. This means that part of what we traditionally call leisure is given a different content.

Much of today's leisure sector is affected by a kind of public service thinking, an effect of municipalisation and professionalisation in this area too. Leisure on a local scale is offered as a finished product right from the start. Both children and adults are served up with ready-made leisure activities. They become consumers of leisure and culture. But people should be able to look after their leisure and cultural environments to a much greater extent. Leisure and cultural activities then become a result of people coming together and co-operating. A much larger proportion of public resources must in future be devoted to this rather than to expensive local authority service complexes and the local authority's own leisure and culture organisation.[35]

Leisure activities available today are also strictly divided on an age basis.[36] This is unfortunate. Many activities ought to be organised on a family basis or in other ways, so that children and adults can work together. But there must also be activities where

123

children can get away from adults. Adolescents have a legitimate need to do things on their own and develop their own culture. This is best done by letting them take responsibility for a certain activity, for premises or such like, within their own associations.

Leisure has become extremely commercialised, not least affecting children and adolescents. Their life is characterised greatly by possessions and mass-media products. At the same time several studies show that many young people are materially satiated and that they long for better social relations with adults instead. But market forces encourage dreams of consumption. For many young people the dreams never become reality, since they themselves or their parents lack the economic means for 'keeping up'. In times of economic recession, the commercial pressures to buy things is even greater. Often the commercial dominance exists because of the lack of good and inexpensive alternatives in areas where children and adolescents live. Many are therefore drawn to the centres of population and the hearts of the cities. These places are often dominated by commercial and, not infrequently, socially unsuitable facilities-pubs, pin-ball arcades, etc. In many small towns there is hardly anything commercially on offer. Instead the meeting place becomes the street or the town square, which can hardly be called conducive to young people's development. It is, among other things, against this background that local authorities will have to devote even more resources than today, in supporting local initiatives and giving young people positive things to occupy themselves with in the areas in which they live. It is, for example, important that there should be non-commercial, drug-free dance and entertainment facilities in residential areas.

Culture is created in daily existence

Culture includes all the social living patterns within a group or a community. These cultural patterns are borne by everything which people create, not only in work and thought, picture, form and music, but also in the mode of living and of mixing with each other—everything which forms social patterns. Culture is created, preserved, altered and renewed in daily existence.[37] Productive co-operation between people, both adults and children, and between the sexes, is a basic requirement of everyday culture. In this way, *everyday culture* represents all the social events in which we are co-creators and participants.[38]

The state of everyday culture is determined by our general living conditions and environments. But the prospects for co-operation in residential areas are bad. The fragmenting and weakening of everyday existence, whilst individualism as a way of life is being romanticised in commercial products, threatens people's chances of defending and influencing their daily and future conditions. Apart from that, more and more of our common affairs are made the domain of career professionals, making it more difficult for people to get involved in solving the problems they share. All this creates an atmosphere conducive to commercial exploitation which prospers through compensating for deficiencies. The neglect of everyday culture is serious since it is just in everyday reality that we can develop and create our own identity and self-respect. It is in everyday life that culture can best be preserved and protected while also being constantly renewed. Co-operation in daily life vitalises environments for children to develop in.

Much of commercial youth culture encourages the passivity of the onlooker. As opposed to this, everyday culture activates people. Strengthening everyday culture will thus become the most important contribution to creating alternatives to commercial culture. Resistance to commercial dominance will be created in well developed everyday culture and will result in a diminishing need for commercial culture. It will not have the same place in our lives.[39]

Manufactured commercial youth culture is predominant; it has become stronger and stronger as co-operation between people in everyday culture has become weaker.

There are therefore many reasons for reinforcing the culture of our daily lives. The worse the conditions for everyday human existence become, the easier it is for commercial culture to dominate everyday life too, and the weaker our resistance to its bad aspects becomes. Reinforcing everyday culture will mainly be a matter of carrying through what we have called the caring economy and caring production, with its mainstay in the local community, and in which children and adolescents will participate. Many people would be involved in working for social and cultural change. Of course, responsibility for more traditional cultural activities, such as drama, music, movement and film, would also be included in the caring work.

Resistance—part of caring work

Associations and other cultural groups can start up various alternatives to commercial culture. Many initiatives are taken on a local level, but often they find it difficult to survive because of competition from the predominant commercial youth culture. Alternatives often get no support from society, since the groups in question do not fit into the normal criteria for grants and subsidies.[40]

In caring production it would be natural for such initiatives to get economic support, help with premises, etc. Social criticism from these groups should not stop society supporting their activities. There are a vast number of such alternatives which could be developed into a wide and varied resistance against commercial culture.

The role of art as a force of resistance

Artistic culture also finds difficulty in holding its own in competition with commercial culture. Artistic culture is obviously of importance, not least because it enriches everyday life and stimulates people to their own creativity and to express their thoughts and feelings.

Art can help us to reach our most profound thoughts and emotions, make them conscious for us in picture, dance and music. Art and the creations of cultural workers is a liberating force in society and therefore belongs to the struggle against commercial culture.

Relating to what we are calling everyday culture, artistic culture takes a completely opposite stance to the commercial one. If everyday culture is to be strengthened the significance of artistic culture must be asserted. People will feel the need for and will call for artistic culture as the conditions of everyday life are improved.[41]

Commitment to everyday culture entails taking a clear stand on amateurisation, even within the cultural field. At the same time, we have to bear in mind that the situation of the professional cultural workers in our society is far from acceptable. The debate on the need for amateurisation has therefore often been conceived in terms of competing with professional cultural workers for employment. This problem of course, can only be avoided if society takes more responsibility for improving cultural workers' maintenance and working conditions.

We must also emphasise the importance of professionals as human assets in everyday culture.[42] Activities within the caring production of the local community will be carried out by the residents, children, adolescents and adults, all in co-operation. But professional cultural workers will play an important role. They can give people the courage and the will to be creative themselves. Giving guidance and teaching different techniques will be an important task for cultural workers. Society must reward cultural workers for being able to take on such tasks. Professional artists cannot be expected to contribute their skills to caring work if their income is not guaranteed by secure employment.

Obviously, as regards the decoration of school premises or other public facilities, residents, pupils or other groups would participate in the planning and the execution of the task, as part of their caring work. But it is just as obvious that such work cannot be carried out without the guidance of professional cultural workers and craftsmen, from the painting and decorating trades for instance.

People's own creativity, within pictorial art, music, film and drama, will become one important part of caring production. But it is important to emphasise that this amateurism, like other productive work within the caring economy, shall be based upon *giving* and *taking* and not upon *buying* and *selling*. This is to say, 'artistic production' in the caring economy will not be created to compete with the artistic output of professional cultural workers on the open market.

The caring economy organised in association form

Popular movements form part of the foundations of Swedish democracy. They are democratic environments, they perform valuable services in society, they can influence the social establishment and they generally have an ideological basis.

We have described how the operating conditions of the popular movements in our society have been made more difficult. Among other things this is because of the impoverishment of local environments and becuse of shifts in population but also because of changes in the working methods of the movements. There is a great deal of interest in clubs among young people, especially where sports clubs and activity groups are concerned, while ideological organisations find it difficult to attract young people to their demands for social change. The child and youth organisations of today have difficulties with their basic principles above all else. There is no lack of interest in politics and social questions among young people, but few are affiliated to any political organisation.

The strength of a popular movement lies in the fact that its demands for social change have an ideological basis, with criticism of the existing social developments, and with promises of something new and better.[43] Popular movements can offer social fellowship. Involvement in a club can give added meaning to the adolescent years, a meaning which is formed by blending struggle with companionship. Club activities give young people a formative environment, where co-operation with each other and between the generations provides a basis for what, in other contexts, we would call social reproduction, that is, looking after and transmitting values, norms and morals from generation to generation. In a club, children and adolescents can take *responsibility* and create their own environments. Clubs could function as alternative environments to the range of leisure and culture offered commercially. This is the ideal. Unfortunately, reality does not always turn out like this.

People have to organise themselves if they are to influence society.[44] It seems that existing strong groups find it easier than the weaker groups to use associations as a platform for promoting their

128

demands. Of all those who are involved in club activities, especially where sport is concerned, women are clearly under-represented compared to men. Most clubs, apart from sports clubs, have unrepresentative distribution as regards social groupings. The middle and upper classes are over-represented compared with the working classes: the same applies with those who are involved as leaders in youth organisations. Young people living in a difficult social situation cannot be expected to seek support in, or fight for change in, club activities. But some organisations have made great contributions to areas which were considered very difficult.

Changes during the past few years have been staggering. Technical development could almost be said to have run wild. Production has become more and more efficient, rationalised and large-scale. This, in turn, has influenced the content of work and also our daily lives.

The new society is becoming more and more difficult to understand and to influence. Political discussions often have to start from things quite different from the specific problems of people's own housing areas, of the neighbourhoods. It is, in the first instance, those who are well educated and those who dare to speak out about difficult social questions who can make themselves heard; many do not think themselves capable of political debate. The old male domination is still present, but in more refined forms. The political language which might be used to liberate, make people aware and make united demands, can also be used to suppress.

There is a risk of young people being trained, at an early age, to acquire the 'correct' roles and the 'correct' language, when they are taught debating at school. Such social climbing does not develop fellowship and solidarity. It represses and distorts important emotional sides of the personality.

The local environments of early industrial society could create movements which were born out of the common experiences of their members, in fact this was the very reason for the associations being formed. The popular movements, therefore, met the needs of the people. The members literally built the new society; people turned out to a man to build community centres, village halls co-operative shops, libraries, etc.

Today's society is very different. The market has refashioned our society from its base. People have had to split up. New environments often lack social events. People from very different backgrounds now find themselves neighbours. The welfare system has cleared away many of the reasons for the struggles of the popular movements. Privatisation stands in the way of collective work; isolation, separations, the disintegration of families likewise. Much of the criticism directed towards the popular movements hits the wrong person. The terms under which the popular movements work have been affected by the social changes of the past few decades, by population movement and by impoverished housing areas. It would be unfair to blame the popular movements for this development and for the social problems in many housing areas. These have not been planned and built in consultation with the associations. In spite of this, the associations are expected to solve these problems. The public sector now deals with much of what the popular movements took on in the old society; but public service policy, which allows housing areas to be erected and completed without the involvement of the residents or local associations, which allows meeting places, shops, leisure facilities and cultural amenities to be prefabricated, is fundamentally at odds with the old traditions of the popular movements. Our society is being confronted with great problems. Disillusion and worry about the future is expressed most clearly by the young and the old. The old guard of the popular movements have seen their ideals become bureaucracy and paralysis, and many young people do not see any point in working within the popular movements. In this situation many associations have become involved with campaigns for new membership, and with meetings for the sake of meetings, and the association has been used as a career ladder. Popular movements need people, but do people need the popular movements?

Our answer to that question is obviously—yes. It is necessary for associations to be allowed to play a considerably larger role in the society of the future. Many of our suggestions and ideas are really based on a very genuine tradition of the popular movements; that people take responsibility for important parts of the running of the community, by organisation and unity. But this demands self-critical discussion by the present day associations, of their forms of work, and that new types of associations are accepted and supported.[45]

For democracy to function, the groundwork of the associations must be developed, vitalised and politicised. Our studies indicate that the association leadership today see themselves more as social administrators than as arbiters of social change. This is partly because the state is making more and more use of the associations where leisure activities for children and adolescents are concerned.[46]

The associations must discuss and reconsider their working methods. It is important to take a stand on such questions as the way in which language is used, the form of meetings, male domination, whether everyone joins in discussions, which groups are reached, etc. Such developmental work ought to be supported by society.

The associations will form the foundations for social change. Caring work ought, above all, to be organised in the form of associations. These could be affiliated to various popular movements—tenants' associations, sports clubs, political societies, etc. It will be associations which will own and run cultural centres, bookshop cafés, restaurants, workshops, cultivation of some crops, shops, etc. Various associations could often work together on a project. There could also be co-operation between the local authority and the associations; e.g. in things concerning certain cultural and leisure facilities.[47]

A change in the local community directed at promoting a caring economy and caring production would also result in more active associations. When the responsibility for common affairs is returned to the residents in a neighbourhood, there will be some point in getting organised to run the activities and to influence development. Public resources must be distributed to support local environments. These resources ought mainly to be channelled through the local network of associations. Local authorities ought to be responsible for distributing funds, but the execution of the work should be in the hands of those who live and work in the areas in question.

For our strategy to work, there should be no further cut-backs in aid to associations. On the contrary, savings made in this area could have disastrous consequences and in the long term would produce higher social cost through greater rejection.

One problem in the operations of the present popular movements is that their work has too often been divided into different age-groups. Many popular movements now have child and youth sections which are separate from the parent organisation. The popular movements ought to be in the forefront of more age-integrated activities. This would happen best by creating, wherever possible, associations in which children, adolescents, adults and the elderly could all be included and would together undertake the various enterprises of caring production.[48]

Another important point, if associations are to be able to function within the caring economy, is that they should have access to *premises*. This question of premises is often difficult for associations and independent groups to solve. There must be opportunities, within every local environment, for active associations and groups to carry out their projects. Many associations could, to their mutual advantage, share in and co-operate over a centre for associations and for cultural activities. Present premises for leisure, schools, etc, will have to be utilised in a better way. Schools, play schools, sports and leisure facilities could also be used for cultural activities during the periods when they are not in normal use. The associations in an area could own premises of various kinds in conjunction with the local authority. This could come about by jointly creating a foundation or a co-operative.[49]

Local associations within a neighbourhood ought to be able to have access to their own premises, where they could have their ordinary meetings and study activities. These premises could easily be fitted into existing housing areas, and they should be free of charge.

The economic community house

A well-developed caring economy will both influence and function along with the other economic systems in our social economy. In this section, we shall mainly summarise some points concerning the relationship of the caring economy with the public sector. Can we talk of a third point of view in the debate on the public sector? We can compare the caring economy to the ground floor of an economic community house, to illustrate relationships with the remaining economic systems.

THE THIRD POINT OF VIEW

In many areas, our society finds itself in a disquieting situation. Many conventional solutions involve demands for a more rationalised and efficient market economy, which in turn results in greater movement of population, and in more people being placed outwith the labour market; there is increased social rejection, more people are prematurely retired, there is an increased dependence on the outside world, continued regional and local impoverishment and increased pressure on the environment and natural resources.

The welfare state's security system—health care, care of children, treatment of addicts and care of the environment—is inadequate. The cost of social rejection threatens to exceed the resources which the public sector has at its disposal to assist and rehabilitate people to a tolerable life.

The public sector is at the centre of debate. Can taxes be raised? Can the public sector deal with the problems which exist now and which will arise in the future? Can the public sector be extended? And, if so, how? Opinions are divided between and within the prevailing political ideologies.

There are many models for the future, many combinations. It is surely no exaggeration to say that we are, in many areas, faced with highly important choices for our future. A projection of today's trends offers, for many people, the most threatening image of the future—that is, continued economic stagnation while social costs due to social rejection rise.

We have discussed how the changes within care, social aid and training are connected with new scientific and political definitions of important areas of society; how social reproduction and everyday life have been neglected in the political visions and the scientific theories. This has hit children hardest of all, since everyday life is their most important sphere of existence. Socially impoverished environments where little happens, shortcomings in care, in attention and in training are a few effects of this situation. The social basis of reproduction has been changed. More and more voluntary caring work has become paid work. That has changed the basic foundations of reproduction. We have questioned whether all work of caring and attention is suited to being salaried employment.

An important trend is that public caring work has become influenced by the model of the market economy with demands for disciplining of time, for efficiency, for saving on resources and for large units. But it takes time and personal, emotional and moral involvement to keep people together and in a collective group which, after all, according to our definition is the basis for all caring work, while work within the market economy most often has quite different characteristics.

Another development which we have described is the professionalisation of care and social aid. This is a question more and more of science defining what social skill is. Old experiences, everyday competence which has been attained by practical work or learning through the old master-apprentice relationships is no longer accepted as skill. The professions have taken over the monopoly of the definition of skill.

The definition of social problems has also changed. Science has, among other things, introduced all sorts of perversions and divergences from the norm; phenomena and behaviour which have been looked upon as normal in other historical periods or in other cultures, have been declared unhealthy. This also means that social problems have seldom been defined in political or moral terms. We are left with a scientific moral code and professional superiority which are very different from the mutual regard which grows out of a functioning social network which strengthens fellowship.

The whole model which the welfare and caring work of the authorities is based upon is largely geared towards public service. This reduces and undervalues people's own involvement and skills. It could lead to a dangerous social climate where personal involvement is not used for changing and improving society. Society takes the supreme responsibility and people do not believe that they are able or allowed to influence, give training, take responsibility, carry out idealistic work. The experiences which create the desire to take responsibility, to influence, to work democratically, are not woven into people's daily lives. For many, it feels more comfortable to free themselves from their responsibilities simply by paying their taxes.

Can a caring economy change the situation in any way? Yes, in many ways, but other measures and 'crisis programmes' are obviously needed too, in order to get to grips with many of the present economic problems. The caring economy will perhaps have greatest effect on the public sector: in many ways it may lead to a re-organisation of this sector.

By better social planning and a conscious policy, it must be possible, in small communities, for people to take responsibility for practical solutions to problems affecting them most. Individual people and groups must be allowed to take part themselves in the caring work and the production of goods and services in an environment to which they are able to relate. When these joint productive activites are built upon they, in turn, create environments where things are happening, where children and adolescents can be given duties and tasks. There is always something for everyone to do, something for the common good, which others can share in too. These tasks have some point; people do things together, build things together and conserve things together. We will again 'turn out to a man' to construct and protect social life, ourselves. People will feel solidarity through common effort and everyone will be useful. Even if the work does not last longer than one hour per day, or is small in a material sense, it will have an immeasurable human value.

Can this really influence and change the present public sector? Can we talk of a 'third point of view' in the debate on the public sector? The strong and secure society which distributes common resources equally, and which does not accept social rejection, should not be disarmed, but many of its present working methods must be changed. This social renewal should be organised, above all, so that people gain control and responsibility over their daily existence, and that children and adolescents have a set place in this everyday society.

Is this possible? Can children and adolescents participate in community work? More and more people are beginning to argue that it is not only possible but totally essential; that children who grow up without having to take responsibility, without participating, without being taken seriously, cannot function in society when they become adults. Children must learn that they have both rights and obligations and that democratic working methods have to be practised by giving children the opportunity to participate in work.

We shall now summarise some of the most important points regarding the relationship of the caring economy with the public sector.

1   In the long term, caring work means de-professionalisation and de-institutionalisation. So, among other things, the handicapped, the elderly and other groups which today have to rely on institutional support shall, as far as possible, be able to function outside in the community, since the social network in which they are included shall have the opportunity and resources, etc, to offer its services. This will imply mutual dependence: and everyone will be able to make their own contributions to collective caring work. Elderly people will do work based on their own terms and interests, and children and adolescents will learn useful work.

2   Caring for and bringing up children will be restored to people who live around and near children. More adults will feel responsibility for childcare and will gain practical opportunities to participate in work within the caring sector. Adults with children of their own will be able to work together with their own and other people's children. Adults with no children of their own will be able to make a great contribution and will perceive how working with children gives their lives greater significance and experience.

3   Caring work will make unpaid, voluntary work appreciated. Idealistic work in associations, co-operatives, etc, will be given great human value. Each individual will have a right and an obligation to participate in caring work of this kind.

4   Caring work will alter the public sector's model of service. If people, so far as possible, are responsible themselves for common affairs, the efforts of the public sector will, in turn, be relieved and complemented. Common affairs, which in some way or other *can* be solved within the caring sector, will become part of voluntary

community work. Social problems will not always be left up to 'society', each local community will try to solve social problems collectively, with support from the public sector. The public sector will have, on the other hand, an environment and a resource to collaborate with.

5 New local social control growing out of this collaboration will set new limits. A caring economy which takes responsibility for its local community environment will make demands on those working there. The adult-child relationship will gain a different moral relevance. This will not be just a disjointed relevance: it will grow out of common experience and collaborative work. The caring society will not accept the establishment of commercial forces or socially unsuitable environments in the local community. The caring economy will set necessary limits on the market.

6 A democracy of involvement will politicise social questions. It will stimulate people to look for new skills, to develop political talents, and to look for political solutions. It will add a new dimension to democracy and make more people participate in political decision-making.

7 Among other things, caring work will build upon the traditional concept of the popular movements and on the need to take responsibility for and to construct one's own environment. This, too, will counter the service mentality, municipalisation and commercialisation. *Constructing* one's own environment will also mean taking the responsibility for entertainment facilities and cultural activities etc.

8 The caring economy will be a decentralised sector. It will pick out the local social aspects of everyday life, presently ignored. It will be based on demands that the community should be easy for all, including children, to relate to. It will not accept environments and activities where participation cannot be incorporated.

9 Caring work will build upon a total conception of what are good formative environments for children. It will not accept the splitting up of social life into many different sectors and areas.

Efforts within one area to improve children's formative conditions, must not be bulldozed in favour of efforts in another area.

10 Caring work opposes privatisation and individualisation. Its collective forms of collaboration open closed doors in the relationships between families, relatives and neighbourhoods. It constructs new friendly and emotional relationships which involve both security and responsibility.

11 Caring work will mean savings, in the long term, for the public sector economy in the form of decreasing social rejection, less vandalism and destruction, more psychological well-being, better quality of life, etc.

12 Caring work will re-assess skills and resources. The products of work will not be valued simply in monetary terms. It will utilise forgotten everyday skills and pass them on to the generations to come.

13 Commitments to a caring economy will lead to a transcending of the private in order to attain co-operation and extended solidarity. As we gain experience from working together, more and more of us will constantly enjoy producing something and creating something which is clearly useful, to oneself, one's own family and other families one has contact with. It will not be so important to devote oneself to acquiring things one needs oneself, since many of these things will exist in the local community. Even one's own domestic production will be able to increase when the opportunity arises for getting help and access to means of production belonging to the caring economy. In other areas things which today belong first and foremost to the private household will be transferred to the caring system, such as growing summer vegetables or organising leisure activities in housing areas.

14 The unpaid work done in the private household and traditionally carried out by women can in many areas be re-organised within the caring economy. In this way time will be spared and we will create better contact between people who have earlier been isolated in their individual apartments. In this way the caring economy will lessen isolation and create greater equality.[50]

138

15   In a number of areas there will be an improved method of collaboration between the public and the caring system.[51] The public sector plans and administrates education, premises for cultural activities and the care of children and old people. If there is a caring economy the public sector will have an environment to work in co-operation with. School, culture, health care authorities will be able

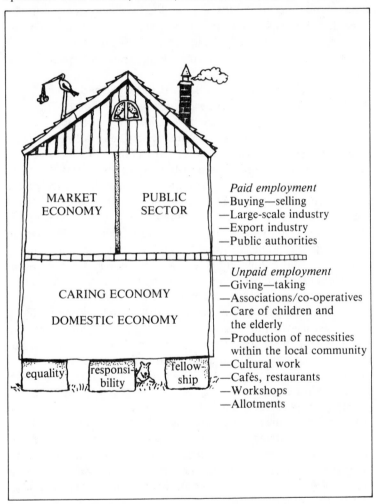

The economic community house

to help towards organising activities which residents themselves are responsible for and where children and adults work together on important projects.

The 'ground floor' in this community house is founded on a caring economy and caring production. This production is based on participation, fellowship, equality, responsibility and tasks for children, adolescents, adults and the elderly. The work is essentially unpaid. It consists of constant giving and taking. Many of those who are today employed within the public sector are needed for effecting a change, towards people taking greater responsibility for their collective affairs. There will, therefore, be permanent staff, mainly concerned with guidance. Participating in caring work, production of goods and services for giving and taking, is the very essence of being a whole person, a fellow human being, a prerequisite for development, identity, fellowship, etc. All people must be able to have this as their base. On the ground floor, we also house the domestic economy and the work carried out there. As described above, the caring economy will also alter much of the isolation of private households. In the 'upper floor' comes the specialisation of the market economy or the public system, that is to say, paid employment within larger scale industrial production or within public administration. Production in the market economy is founded on buying and selling. The upper floor provides important extra opportunities for people, in the form of specialisation, involvement and efficient production for the export market, for instance. It provides material security for the community, a varied assortment of goods and services, plus education and research with funds from the public sector. If some of the surplus from the market economy is distributed to the caring production of the public sector, specialised production will also become an advantage for everyone.

One great problem today is that the upper floor, especially with regard to economic resources, has developed to too great an extent, at the expense of the ground floor, and suffocates life there. We must therefore strive for a better balance between the caring economy on the one hand, and the market economy and the public economy on the other, to make noticeable, to re-appraise and to restore the forgotten sector.[52]

Drawbacks and problems

We should not however indulge in a rosy, romantic piece of wishful thinking, about a society which is unattainable. The road to a functioning caring economy is long; the old adage that society will never be completely finished probably applies here. Each community, each generation, must be able to build and create its *own* society. One cannot just accept existing solutions. A true democracy where *everyone* participates is, in addition, a very hard-working democracy. Work and decision-making will take up considerably more time than we are used to in the efficient society. Ideology will be confronted with ideology, skill with skill. The caring economy will be a democracy full of conflict but nevertheless vibrantly alive. However, a number of unanswered questions stand in line for discussion.

Among other things, we must ask ourselves how the world around us will react to a transition to an economy which is directed more towards caring production. How will other countries react, those with whom we have trade and cultural links; how will our own industrial sector act? Or will opposition be greatest from the present public economy?

Even if it will only be unfounded speculation, we ought to outline some possible problems and obstacles for the caring economy. This is important if we are to have a realistic basis for action and for directing our reforms towards combatting the obstacles. It is a question of obstacles both within the structure of our society and within the human psyche.

1 Technical development and research are, in the first instance, geared to the demands of the market economy. Very little research concerns what we might call alternative or small-scale production for local requirements. Obviously, this impedes movement towards strengthening the local community's caring production. A functioning caring economy is not a concept opposed to technical progress. On the contrary, technical research is necessary to test alternative forms of production.

2 We are confined by the restrictions of international economics. Our economy is bound up with high levels of imports and exports.

Multinational corporations have a great deal of power in Sweden, too. Whatever guise development assumes, regarding Sweden's dependence on trade with the outside world, there is the suspicion that strongly commercial forces, both at home and abroad, will look uneasily upon Sweden, if social experiments are indulged in, and thereby threaten their commanding position.

3   We may suspect that even Swedish commercial life will apply the brake. The market economy is based, in many respects, upon the existence of an affluent population which satisfies more and more of its requirements by greater consumption. An advanced caring economy, where more and more people see contributing to caring work as the most important aim in their lives, which gives life greater meaning, in many ways threatens the ideal picture created by the market economy. The compensatory role of consumption decreases proportionately with the extent to which the individual participates and finds an important role and responsibility. The caring economy takes time, interest and resources from the market, especially in relation to children and adolescents, for whom consumption is one of their most important functions today.

4   People will themselves collectively produce more and more of those goods and services which would otherwise have been commercial market consumption. Obviously this is another threat to the market. It must be expected that the proponents of the market will react negatively. They will probably try to counteract the ideas behind the caring economy with all the means at their disposal. Among other things, there is a risk that the marketing of consumer goods will be made even more seductive, by portraying even greater illusions of the need to escape the duties and responsibilities of reality. Consumption could still be promoted as an alternative to the banalities of everyday life.

5   But we can also imagine quite the opposite reaction, i.e. that caring work will be incorporated into the market sphere. There is a danger that the market, just as so many times before, will have perceived, well in advance, people's need of and wish for a smooth-running everyday existence, which increases the risk that all the caring work and activities will be commercialised. The caring sector could become a new market to be exploited.

6   Like many other countries, Sweden is experiencing economic problems of stagnation, high unemployment, closure of industries, large foreign debt, few or no pay rises, price and rent increases, while the public sector is cut back for lack of funds. In that situation there is a risk of the caring economy being considered a much too naive and unrealistic idea—a beautiful pipe-dream devoid of political or economic reality. Shortsighted economic planning in a difficult economic climate seldom has room for any social changes; but meanwhile, the public costs rise *and* the future is put in balance.

7   The idea of expenditure cuts is a serious threat. In contrast to what might happen, according to point number 6, the caring economy might, myopically, be considered a chance to cut expenditure in the public sector. In times of economic austerity it seems to have become a 'sport' to look for savings within the public sector. Savings are almost impossible in many areas. A large number of resources have already been tied up for many years in expensive facilities whose costs one cannot ignore. The only areas where savings work are, for example, in subsidies for associations, in staff costs, in opening times for local authority service facilities. In the light of this, the caring economy might perhaps be welcomed by those who want to cut back on as much of the public sector as possible. In that case, the old charitable organisations will return, which, like the old philanthropists will 'save' those worst situated. At the same time, these eager savers will argue, we can escape costs for permanently employed staff in the social aid and caring services. We have, in many places, already made it clear just how far from our thoughts such an argument is.

8   Will the caring economy become a 'therapeutic island'? Whilst we agree to the caring economy and its positive action, the market economy will resist change in the work and the production which it carries out. There is even a risk that certain people could agree to the caring economy in order to escape discussing changes within the market economy. This means that it would seem easier to accept hard low-paid work, if daily life was full and rich. We have argued that people cannot live two lives. Changes in the market economy and the work done there are also necessary for the caring economy to function.

9   There are many who do not believe that people will join in caring work. We are too comfortable, do not want to take responsibility, are only interested in our own personal well-being. This has been reported by different surveys, about the de-politicising and privatisation which characterises many housing areas, even those where no social problems seem to exist. Many people see the beautiful façades as proof that they have succeeded in life, though they do not see or do not want to see the problems that exist, and that their children are faring badly. Advanced stages of rock-solid protectionism exist in some areas, forcing children out of the well-developed areas. In such areas there is a danger that neither children nor adults will join in caring work, at least not where it entails working on projects which are not directly in one's own personal interests but which are for the common good. It would, for example, mean that no-one would get a drop in working hours, if the new leisure time had to be linked with collective caring work. This demands far-reaching changes in attitude. One experience has been that if children are allowed to learn the importance of working together, the attitude of the whole family is affected.

10   There is a great risk that it will be principally women who will take responsibility for caring work, even in its new forms, and that men will choose to remain uninvolved. Instead men will come to work even harder within the other sectors where paid work dominates. But it is important for many reasons that men join in. Far too many children spend far too little time with their fathers and other men. Children need to have good contact with men. Caring work can give this kind of opportunity, which would be good for the development of the children and of the men.

11   Will those who do join in lose financially? This problem mainly concerns industrial workers. One cannot leave work to participate in caring work, without there being complications regarding both production and workmates, even if this were to become a basic right. The same problem arises at the present time, concerning the right of union leaders—as recently proposed—to take time off for school activities. The same argument might arise even within the body of civil servants in the public sector. Those wishing to get on in their careers cannot reduce their work

commitments to take part in caring work. These problems provide further argument that practical problems must be solved and that caring work must be considered not only a right but also an obligation.

12 Will the caring economy reinforce class barriers? Certain people think that a caring economy would run the risk of being beneficial only to the strong sections of society, that those who already live in strong social positions will be much more eligible for also taking on further tasks in their local communities, while weak areas become even weaker. Various surveys also show that the public sector is suspicious of the weak areas. They assume that it will not be possible to start any caring work in socially problematic areas, or that the municipal authorities will have to go into the weak environments and organise activities from the start. This would entail strong environments getting greater participation and collective responsibility for social questions, while the weak areas would be dominated by local authority commitment. This strengthens the feeling that there must be strong political control of community resources, towards those areas and groups in which the need for support is greatest, but also that these contributions shall, in the first instance, be directed towards supporting efforts from the residents themselves and combating municipalisation.

13 In contrast to what has been said in point number 12, there is also a risk that those who live in what we would define as strong and fortunate areas will consider that the idea of caring work might be good, but that 'it doesn't concern us', only the weak groups.

14 Would the existing associations not be able to cope with an increase in workload or pressure? This would make impossible a caring economy, which is based so much on the concept of associations. Certain associations might not be interested in building up a movement which is based on the participation of everyone if, for example, they advocate contest and the competitive spirit. We can still argue that the caring economy would strengthen and develop the body of associations and the form of associations as a method of democratic co-operation.

15   Caring work will hopefully lead to a politicisation of social problems and collective affairs. But many people will probably see this in a negative light. In various surveys it has been shown that, among other things, the present political institutions often feel threatened, and try to slow down or even stop attempts at change when it appears that those who participate make uncomfortable political demands.[53]

16   The 'public service mentality' has led to many people feeling uncertain about taking initiatives themselves. Children and adolescents are not used to being considered important assets in society. Many people will demand ready-made solutions and models and will expect the public sector's representatives to have all solutions at hand. But the activities must be able to emerge from local initiatives. Ideas should not be handed 'down from on high'.

17   The public sector's distribution of resources can become too bureaucratic, complicated and muddled. This favours resourceful groups, who have had practice in writing applications, communicating and holding discussions with the authorities, etc. Municipal authorities will have to find non-bureaucratic and simple ways of supporting experiments and activities. Strong local authority organisation could counteract blanket solutions. But we must avoid territorial rivalries between various authorities caused by lack of co-operation between sectors.

18   Those who work within the public sector today, and especially those who have undergone a long course of training to work with other people's problems, might wish to curb any move towards a caring economy. We have already discussed the negative effects of professionalisation. A change in attitude is required among the so-called experts, but also so that the skills and experience of the present professionals are utilized in education, guidance, etc.

19   Caring work could be divisive both for those who are to participate in order to learn, and for those who are to receive the support. Continuity in the enterprise is thus important. This means, for example, that pupils who are given work within child-care and the care of the elderly must be allowed to follow the

progress of the children or the elderly, for at least one term. This also means that the enterprise cannot be allowed to be made dependent upon the sporadic donation of subsidies. An association or co-operative which enters into a project must be able to depend on getting support for many years to come.

20   Social changes take a long time and we are often impatient when it comes to seeing results from effort put in. The caring economy could be difficult for some people to accept—those who want quick results and do not wish to wait to see the social and economic gains of the future. But in this case, these people do not see that local environments contain large unexploited resources, which, if used to advantage, will give tangible social and environmental effects even if it might take a long time.

Social planning for the caring economy

The caring economy must evolve from people's involvement and local requirements. State, municipal and regional authorities ought not to closely control the activities from on high. Instead, the role of society ought to be, as far as possible, to clear away obstacles so that caring production can function, and to support endeavours economically or in the form of premises.

Strengthening local environments and building up activities there, renewing social life and making people more involved in the running of their local environment, is one of the most important measures for creating better formative conditions for children and adolescents, and thereby also opposing the dominance of commercialism. If this is to be carried through, there must be conscious social planning, based on the objective of strengthening local neighbourhoods. This also demands a political channelling of community resources towards activities in those areas and among those groups where need is greatest. The aim must be that resources shall be divided as equally as possible among the various local environments. This is not to imply that all local environments are to look alike or that activities are to be run in the same way everywhere. On the contrary, within this framework there is enough scope for a very versatile programme of activities.

Many of the final decisions regarding local environments today lie beyond the control of the community. This concerns economic conditions, power, etc. For example, it is impossible to plan for good local environments in a place where the future face of local industry is uncertain. Which places of work will there be? How many people will be forced to move to other towns? Will there be continued depopulation? Even if we disregard these fundamental planning problems, other means of control must be created if we are to obtain better local environments. The most important planning must lie with the local authorities. On the municipal level, co-operation between committees must increase. Within civic authorities, leisure boards could be given the main responsibility for strengthening local environments. Leisure boards could then be changed to 'local environment committees', whose main task ought to be maintaining and distributing public sector subsidies to caring production.

LOCAL ENVIRONMENT COMMITTEES

It is important that decisions are made as close to the people as possible. There may have been good reasons for introducing larger municipal authorities, but the system has had many disadvantages. One such disadvantage is that the number of people involved in local government has dropped; a second, that decisions have been taken further and further away from the people and the environments they live in; a third, that professionalisation has increased. By a resolution of 1980, municipal authorities were able to set up local bodies for the school, social, leisure and culture spheres. The most common thing is that district committees have been introduced to this end. It would be unfortunate if we also got division and sectorisation on the local plane. It would be possible to introduce departmental boards or local bodies for the so-called human relations committees, even if few local authorities have done so.

The right of decision, in a number of questions which touch upon the local community, can be decentralised further. In the long term, each local authority ought to be able to introduce *local environment committees* (in local environments of 200–400 households). There ought not to be any division into different sectors here. The local environment committees could have the following duties:

1   to co-ordinate caring work in the local environments—to distribute the economic support to different groups, associations, co-operatives: but not to start their own activities
2   to co-ordinate economic contributions to caring production and the caring economy, from state and municipal authorities
3   to be responsible for the co-ordination of premises and utilisation of premises in the area
4   to be responsible for environmental protection and the conservation of the area.

Local environmental committees could naturally be nominated in various ways. However, it would be advantageous if they were chosen by *direct* ballot. During a trial period, different combinations could be tested.[54]

RESEARCH

The changes we suggest are mostly of the sort which demand a research and development programme, regarding questions both of method and of organisation. An extensive research programme should be carried out and evaluated. The object of the developmental work should be to test different ways of strengthening local environments, of creating better conditions for the young to grow up in, of contributing to social renewal, of developing caring production and a caring economy, of opposing commercialism and of developing the work of associations locally.

Many of the ideas which we have presented here are, to a certain extent, being tried out today, others demand more thorough research. Research programmes are often very diffuse and badly co-ordinated. It is important to develop and to give people and groups the time and resources to apply themselves to this developmental work.

Both state and municipal authorities have a huge responsibility to support this action in different ways. The research programmes ought to be conducted in a representative number of local authority districts.

Developmental work requires resources, but this does not necessarily mean that community expenditure as a whole has to rise because of these contributions. It is above all else a question of better co-ordination and of revising priorities for community resources. There are, for example, a number of various odd forms of support for action similar to the developmental work we had envisaged. These ought to be co-ordinated and used in the research programme. Among other things, it would be a question of creating alternative production of both goods and services, and social care. This is what we have called, collectively, caring production. The community's commitment to this caring economy is very small today, while the state's contributions of public funds, to production in the market economy, amount to a multi-million sum. Among other things, it is important to reappraise parts of this support to the caring economy.

Making a start

Those changes of which we are talking are usually of such a kind that we can hardly describe their progress in a survey report. Some people have criticised the report *Ej till salu* for not having any cut and dried proposals. People want to see tangible steps forward on the road to a new society. But changes based upon human involvement have to evolve from local initiatives, local needs, local resources and local ideas. If we adopt these fundamental thoughts, it would actually be wrong to present a cut and dried set of proposals which would be implemented 'from top to bottom'. On the other hand, we naturally maintain that there are problems and obstacles which require certain centralised decisions.

A STRATEGY AT COMMUNITY LEVEL

In the short term the most important thing is that parliament, the government, local authorities, political parties, organisations, etc, agree to the main idea. This is obviously imperative if we are to progress towards a functioning caring economy. The present situation of persistence in denying its existence and practically hindering its development, cannot continue. We must therefore accept certain commitments about the future:

☐ Agreeing to a caring economy does not imply, and cannot be allowed to imply, that society can determine the details of its development. On the contrary, it must be allowed to evolve without outside control, apart from in one instance, which has already been dealt with. This requires the desire to share out community resources to the areas and the groups where the need for investment is greatest.

☐ Agreeing to a caring economy means being open to development and research. This is why a research programme in a number of local authority areas is so important, in order to try out different models and solutions for a relatively long period. The power of example can be immense.

☐ Agreeing to a caring economy is a matter of trying to clear away obstacles and problems which exist, or which will come into existence in the future in order to oppose the realisation of the philosophy of caring. This might mean necessary changes in legislation, but also support of debate, discussions and educating the public in the main ideas.

A LOCAL AUTHORITY STRATEGY

At the local authority level, agreeing to the caring economy means, principally, supporting changes (based on the caring philosophy) economically and in the form of premises.

A good guideline would be to sound out the interest among residents in an area, in the associations, the schools, etc, as to whether it would be possible to run the enterprises in co-operative form—for example, before a local authority were to start up new enterprises under its own direction.

It also means a change in priorities for the local authority budget, plus improved co-operation and co-ordination, crossing committee boundaries.

Agreeing to a caring economy in a local authority area should also mean that in the local context the local authority will initiate and place the production of those goods and services which are included in local authority operations and which are consumed within the local authority institutions.

For example, this could be various forms of craftsmanship. In this situation community subsidies should be given if the productive enterprise fulfils the requirement that it should be beneficial to the area and also offers children and adolescents the chance to participate in production.

In order to delimit the local environments, the authorities ought to map out the existing natural local environments. This work could result in what we could call a social environmental map. A summary of present or planned population figures for the area, plus the need for places of employment and public service institutions, ought to accompany this map. It is important to try to get a natural mixture of age-groups in the individual local environments.

153

In caring production, the local authorities could encourage experiments with new techniques and ideas for development in production and work. For example, at the instigation of the local authorities, projects could be carried out in conjunction with research workers who have as their brief the research of production techniques which are suitable for caring production in local environments.

A LOCAL ENVIRONMENT STRATEGY

Perhaps the most important areas in our short-term strategy are the local environments in the form of housing areas, areas around schools, etc. Changes can be made progressively. Since one of the ideas is that schools should be linked more closely with the local community, we shall present here an idea on how functioning caring work could come about with initiatives from the school.[55] The same working method could obviously work for a local association which wanted to begin making its contribution to its own local community. The best thing would certainly be if a school class and an association could work together right from the start.

Contact with the local community—one example

Contacts with the local community can come about in many different ways. The school curriculum today already gives quite a lot of scope for personal resourcefulness. It also gives pupils scope to co-operate in the planning of activities. Methods of working ought, of course, to be discussed and decided by pupils and adults together. The best way of initiating a scheme for bringing the school closer to the local community would be to work on various projects. This would be possible in all stages of comprehensive and sixth form education. Most school subjects could be involved in these projects, plus, of course, the subjects which are today called 'free activities'.

154

One could begin by outlining how 'our own' local community looks, its prospects and problems. How much do people who are occupied inside the school really know about the surrounding community? Examples of things which could be investigated are:

☐ Which places of work are there around 'our' school? What is produced? Which problems exist within these places of work? What do the people who work there think? Which occupational groups work there? How are they organised? Which trades unions are there? What do they think of the work, and the values and conditions of that work?

☐ How do the social conditions in 'our' district look? How do social authority workers see 'our' area? What do the police think of it? What deficiencies are there, what could be improved? We should not forget that other generations perhaps see the problems in a different light to us. How do parents and the elderly see their situation? What do they think of young people and their problems?

☐ What does the leisure situation look like in 'our' district? What sort of leisure facilities are there? What happens at after-school centres and recreation centres? What do the people who live here think of the leisure opportunities? What do they do in their free time? What are the deficiencies? What would they like to have? What commercial leisure facilities are there? Are there any good alternatives to these?

☐ Which associations are active in 'our' district? What do they think of life here? Which problems do they have? What would they wish to change? Is there a shortage of any important associations in the district? What could this depend on?

☐ What is the housing situation like? Is there enough housing? How do different groups live? What do residents think of their living conditions? What does the tenants' association think? The private residents' association? Who owns the houses? Who determines the rents? The prices of private housing, etc?

☐ What cultural opportunities are there? What sort of films are shown in our cinemas? What selection would we like to have? What sort of music is on offer? What opportunities are there for making music oneself or for entering into other cultural activities? How do we perceive the influence of the commercial youth culture?

There are certainly many more questions which could be included in an outline of 'our' community, its possibilities and problems. The greater the problems which exist in local environments, which are not treated by the school, the more alienated pupils will become from schoolwork. Studying the local community in this way gives both knowledge, awareness and, hopefully, the inspiration to want to be involved and to influence and to change, for example by joining one of the existing associations or by forming new ones.

It would be natural to make contact with and invite visits from representatives of the associations which are active in an area, or to visit them in their own premises. The associations could make their contributions during lessons or during the time for free activities, and in the time before and after the school day. The associations could give information on what they do and how one can become a member, etc. They can also give an insight into important social questions. The pupils could also put questions, have discussions— making use of the knowledge gained from the inventory of their community—and put forward their opinions and make demands.

The participation of the associations in the school, by this method, would principally provide an opportunity for the pupils to get involved in social questions and especially the way in which the local community is run and organised. According to our way of looking at things, their main task would not be to offer children occupations for their free time, in the form of hobbies or other 'therapeutic' activities, but to offer a democratic environment with the chance of having some influence.

When the inventory is finished we ought to ask ourselves whether there is any special activity which we could get involved in. It is here that the school can become a very real asset to the community. We could perhaps start our own projects or co-operate with different associations or the local authorities. The activities might, for example, be a matter of visiting the elderly and the disabled. It might be a matter of conservation and reparation of things which would otherwise have been discarded or destroyed. It might be a matter of decoration, in colour and form, of some local authority premises.

APPENDICES

Summary of proposals concerning caring work and caring production

1 We believe that changes in the market economy are necessary in the long term—among other things, to reduce the social costs which the market economy creates.

2 We suggest that measures should be taken to break the dominance of multinational companies over our economy and culture.

3 We believe that it is necessary to find ways of supporting an alternative, informal economy alongside the market economy, one which has social aims and which is based on voluntary work, service and reciprocal service.

4 We suggest that there should be a reduction in working hours for all employees in either market economy production or the public sector; this reduction would then enable them to participate in caring work.

5 We believe that this reduction should provide time only for working within the caring economy, not for an increase in traditional leisure.

6 We believe that school should have a part to play in the changing of society: together with other sections in the community, it should provide good conditions for child development.

7 We believe that a school must 'open its doors' and co-operate with its local community.

8 We believe that the local community should function as a resource for the school and that the school should function as a resource for the local community.

9 We believe that a most important part of educational policy should be the creation of lively local communities which provide not only favourable environments for child development but also pedagogical resources.

10 We suggest that pupils should, throughout the whole of their elementary schooling and as part of their tuition, undertake productive tasks in the local community; for example, caring work with children and the elderly, or in various forms of work in the local community.

11 We believe that the skills communicated by the schools must be geared more to, and take their point of departure in, those conditions which the pupils encounter in their caring work.

12 We believe that the educative roll of the school can be complemented by pupils being able to meet adults with varying backgrounds and experience, also by pupils taking part in a productive, social life outside school.

13 We suggest that, in the school, pupils together with teachers and other members of staff, should have influence over, and responsibility for,

financial resources affecting, for example, repairs, decoration of premises, purchase of materials, and the joint activities of their own class.

14 We suggest that pupils in both comprehensive schools and sixth-form colleges should take part in the practical work of their school, joining in work-groups dealing with repairs, cleaning, decoration and the care of premises.

15 We suggest that pupils have responsibility for the preparation of food for their own class.

16 We suggest that pupils' associations should have the right to negotiate with the school administration and board of governors.

17 We suggest that pupils should be allowed to appoint ombudsmen in each school.

18 We suggest that a home-classroom should be allocated to each class or group of pupils.

19 We suggest that, in the long term, the home-classroom should be located in the local community—in a flat, private house, farm or other suitable premises.

20 We suggest that tuition groups consisting of pupils from different levels in comprehensive schools are preferable to groups divided under the present system of classes.

21 We suggest that present school buildings ought to be used for the activities of associations and for other cultural purposes.

22 We suggest that pupils' caring work in comprehensive and sixth-form education should account for one day per week or its equivalent.

23 We believe that caring work should be fitted into the full school day.

24 We believe that a three-term system should be tested in Swedish comprehensive and sixth form schools.

25 We suggest that appropriate changes be made in curricula and time-tables so that our suggestions can be implemented.

26 We suggest that a system of continuing education be created, especially for higher year-groups in comprehensive schools and sixth-form colleges.

27 We believe that privatisation of the public sector is incompatible with a close-knit community; personal profit should not be allowed to control care and social aid.

28 We believe that looking after and caring for children is a right and a duty for all, and that provision must be made so that everyone will be able to participate in this caring work.

29 We believe that local authorities ought to take responsibility for creating, in housing areas, productive enterprises which can be run by the residents through their associations.

30 We suggest that rules be formulated for reaching a balance between houses and places of work as the centre of activity for local communities.

31 We believe that local authorities ought to support production in residential areas by providing, among other things, premises and economic stimuli.

32 We believe that local authorities ought to investigate the extent to which, through residents' organisations, the care of children and the elderly, also community activities, health centres, creches, etc. can be organised. Local authorities ought to support such enterprises.

33 We believe that staff concerned with the care of children and the elderly ought to be given more training in instructing groups of pupils in caring work.

34 We believe that everyone, depending on their own conditions and interests, has a duty to join in caring work of various kinds.

35 We suggest that, as an experiment, caring service be made obligatory for both men and women. Everyone will participate in caring work, based on their capabilities, for the equivalent of 2 hours per day. Caring service will be combined with shorter working hours in the commercial and the public sectors.

36 We believe that the professionalisation and institutionalisation of caring work ought to be reduced, to the benefit of various models in which organisations and other local groups will become resources for caring work.

37 We believe that local groups, working in the form of associations, should be given extra resources if they collaborate in an activity for the benefit of the community and in the after-care of those who have been social outcasts.

38 We believe that changing the form of social caring work will change the public sector and thus, apart from the beneficial effect on education, will also give socio-economic advantages.

39 We believe that local authority investment in leisure should principally be directed towards supporting groups and associations which themselves organise various forms of leisure and cultural activities.

40 We believe that leisure activities for mixed age-groups should be given priority.

41 We believe that the local authorities must, to a greater extent than is the case at the moment, support local initiatives which offer alternatives to commercial leisure activities, and which ensure worthwhile activities for young people in the areas where they live.

42   We believe that the present leisure committees in local authorities should be responsible for the mainly local authority co-ordination of caring work in the neighbourhoods. (See also point number 69.)

43   We believe that training for recreation leaders should be designed to fit the requirements and methodology of a functioning local community.

44   We believe that the state and the local authority ought to support the development of the everyday culture of local environments, so that people can themselves, in groups and associations, take responsibility for their own cultural environment.

45   We believe that, within such a development, cultural workers ought to be able to play an important part, individually or in groups, in providing instruction, ideas and support.

46   We believe that, in the experiments within neighbourhoods as suggested above, the development of everyday culture ought to be a dominant feature.

47   We believe that the popular movements are one of the most important environments in which children can grow up. They provide opportunities for taking responsibility and creating one's own environment, and they offer an alternative to the range of commercial leisure and culture activities.

48   We consider that the popular movements should be developed so that being organised in this kind of group is felt to be a means of influencing one's situation.

49   We believe that it is important for each generation to be able to create, construct and reconstruct its own everyday existence. This is best accomplished by means of various associations.

50   We believe that it is important for society, represented by the state and the local authority, to have to remove obstacles which prevent various youth groups from constructing and taking responsibility for their own meeting places.

51   We believe that caring production, as outlined above, should be run and owned by various associations.

52   We believe that greater co-operation between the traditional popular movements and the new 'alternative' movements would be useful.

53   We believe that child, youth and sports organisations should strive to improve their methods of working.

54   We believe that the role of associations in the local community must be strengthened.

55   We believe that this does not remove the need to strengthen central organisations which, *inter alia,* can promote better basic resources.

162

56 We consider that a reinforcement of the groundwork in the associations must involve a self-critical reappraisal of working methods, also greater equality, etc.

57 We consider that in the future, the work of popular movements should also be based on voluntary work. People must be made aware of the risk of professionalisation within the popular movements.

58 We believe that the associations must be careful not to lose their important role as innovators of social change as they take on more community tasks.

59 We believe that the work of local associations must be developed and renewed, *inter alia,* within the framework of the local experimental programmes which we have suggested.

60 We believe that local authorities should draw up plans for the ways in which association meeting rooms and premises for cultural activities should be organised in each local environment.

61 We consider that each local association should have access to their own meeting rooms, free of charge, in their own neighbourhood.

62 We believe that a lively association movement is essential for counteracting commercial domination in children's leisure time and culture.

63 We believe that a functioning local environment, which people can relate to, comprises 200–300 households.

64 We believe that local authorities should examine the possibilities of initiating and placing, in local environments, the production of goods and services which will be used within local authority institutions.

65 We believe that local authorities ought to carry through outline planning of investments in respective local environments. The aim would be to create fairness and equal distribution between different local environments.

66 We believe that local authorities ought to support, by way of economic guarantees and grants, initiatives in those local environments in which encouragement and economic reinforcement are called for.

67 We believe that the balance of local environments requires that there is central and political direction of resources towards those areas in greatest need.

68 We believe that the main responsibility of local authorities is to plan and support local environments.

69 We believe that the boards of leisure ought to be the committees which, in co-operation with other authorities concerned, have greatest responsibility for the planning of the local environment. Boards of leisure should then be reorganised into boards of the local environment. (See also point number 42.)

70   We suggest that local authorities appoint local environment committees to co-ordinate caring work and the economic contributions to caring production, to co-ordinate premises and to be responsible for environmental protection and conservation in the area.

71   We suggest that an extensive experimental programme be carried out to reinforce local environments; to create better conditions for children to grow up in; to create changes in the schools, residential environments and social care; to develop caring work, community service and caring production in order to counteract commercialism and develop the ground work of association activities. Trials ought to be carried out in a representative number of local authority districts with support both from the state and the local authority.

72   We suggest that the Swedish National Youth Council and Child Environment Council be combined in a Local Environment and Child Development Council, in order to co-ordinate, at national level, resources given to model projects and developmental work.

Other measures for creating better formative conditions for children and for counteracting commercialism

The proposal suggested in chapter 4, 'Our Children', should be seen as an attempt at creating better formative conditions for children and thereby also counteracting commercial domination. The report has also discussed other proposals. In this book we have concentrated on the proposal for a caring economy. Therefore in this appendix we shall briefly summarise the remaining proposals. Those who wish to study the thinking and background more closely must turn to the main research work.

1 Culture in working life

It is imperative that the initiatives which have been taken to create cultural activities in working life are pursued. In this way the working environment may be influenced for the better. The fellowship of work could, in a completely different way than at present, become a starting point for building up activities which are based on group experiences and which provide the opportunity to give expression to one's own experiences.

We believe that trades union organisations ought to take the initiative and responsibility for developing the cultural environment in places of work.

2 The adolescents' right to employment

Young people from the age of 16 ought to have the right to employment or further education. It might be of value to enable pupils in younger age-groups to combine education and work. Work ought to be educational. There ought to be tutors in every place of work. Society must, by law, guarantee employment to all young people. Since apprenticeship would be necessary, pay could be lower than on the normal labour market, but the pay should be sufficient to guarantee a set income to the young people concerned.

Companies and authorities must be directed to take a certain number of young people into their workforce. Youth pay ought to be combined with demands placed on the young people, equivalent to the demands placed on other employees. They should pay for their food, in school for instance, and they should have deductions made for absence due to illness and compensation from the social security office, just as with other wage-earners. They should make tax returns, etc.

We suggest that a youth guarantee is introduced, giving all young people, between the ages of 16 and 20, employment within commercial production, the public sector, or education. Young people will receive payment in line with youth pay agreements.

We suggest that young people over 16 should, as a consequence, have the same obligations as other wage-earners, e.g. to make tax returns.

We suggest that the Youth Opportunities Scheme legislation is tightened so that companies and public authorities ore obliged to take on young people.

3   Re-settlement

The depopulation of the countryside has created serious social and cultural effects. Many depopulated local authority areas have an uneven distribution of age-groups. Society ought to support a re-settlement of these areas of depopulation for those who want to move back, perhaps to start a smallish industry or to devote themselves to forestry or agriculture.

We suggest that society should economically support re-settlement of depopulated areas. Above all, youth collectives, associations and co-operatives should be stimulated.

4   Work experience for sixth-form pupils

Younger pupils should take part in caring work because it provides experience, skills and an awareness of the value of work. Periods of practical experience and work, primarily within the market economy or within the public sector, ought to occur also, but mainly for the higher year-groups. Pupils must also learn about the conditions prevailing in the commercial market sector and the public sector. This knowledge will best be gained by way of continuing periods of apprenticeship. At places of work there should be tutors who will give the young people guidance. These tutors should also be able to assist in the school, where pupils will have the opportunity to show their place of study to others, school visits being a suitable part of the caring work of the tutors. For this to be carried out, legislation will be necessary which requires companies and public institutions to take in work-experience trainees from the schools. Trades union organisations must, furthermore, have the right to appoint tutors who have guidance of school pupils included in their job specification.

We suggest that all sixth-form colleges should have continuous periods of work experience.

We suggest that projects for the benefit of the community are introduced in each local authority area to cater for a proportion of the pupils' caring work.

We suggest that the school is given the right of placing sixth-form pupils in apprenticeships within the market economy and within the public sector.

We suggest that trades union organisations, at each place of work, are given the right to appoint tutors who have the guidance of pupils, during the pupils' periods of work experience, included in their job specification.

5 Pupil democracy

Pupil democracy may be developed in many different ways. Our suggestions on the running of the school and on economic responsibility at classroom level are an important prerequisite for this. Most important is that pupils are allowed to co-operate in the daily life of the school. But pupils, like other groups in the school, must also be allowed to influence the more long-term planning and the education policy of the local authority, e.g. by means of a right of negotiation.

We suggest that the pupil associations should be given a right of negotiation with the school administration and board of governors.

6 The school as opposition to commercial dominance

By means of the changes in schools outlined above, pupils will encounter values other than commercial ones. The need for compensatory consumption will decrease. The pupils' existence will become more meaningful. In addition, making pupils aware and critical of the commercial pressure to which they are daily exposed should be part of the school's general education in a number of school subjects, especially social studies, Swedish, etc.

The present curriculum allows for this, but matters concerning the commercial youth culture should be given more prominence in the curriculum.

We believe that the present curriculum should be revised so that time and opportunities are provided to illustrate the content of commercial youth culture, its attractiveness, and alternatives to it.

7 Culture in schools and nursery schools

Greater emphasis should be placed on creative activities in schools and nursery schools, mainly by strengthening and developing, in various ways, the child's powers of self-expression. Pupils should, to a much greater extent, organise various cultural activities themselves—for example, theatre visits and visits to and from cultural workers.

We believe that creative activities ought to be given greater scope in nursery schools, and that new culturally creative activities should be widened in all subjects in the school.

8 Associations in social work

We have pointed out the role of associations in caring work. Society ought to support the social activities of the associations—for example their arrangement of alternative vacation trips.

We believe that local authorities ought to support social activities under the direction of associations in the local environment.

Local authorities ought to support associations which are willing to arrange alternative vacation trips for mixed groups of children and adults.

9 Changed forms of ownership and the struggle against housing speculation

We find it unacceptable that housing has become a commodity for speculation and that tax regulations differ from owning and renting one's home.

We suggest that, in order to prevent private exploitation and speculation, the trade in housing on the open market be limited.

10 Influencing housing locally

Influence for the individual over everyday conditions is the basis of democracy. In each housing area, the residents themselves should, in our opinion, be given direct responsibility for management, repairs and constant maintenance. Increased local control must not, however, undermine the basic residential social aims, such as making rents uniform between old and new areas, and reducing segregation in housing.

We suggest that residents be given the right to self-administration of housing.

11 Housing for adolescents

Many young people have difficulty in finding a suitable place for their first home. Housing planners must take this into consideration when building and renovating housing areas. Collective houses could be one of the solutions.

We believe that the state and local authorities must, in their building and renovating programmes, make allowance for the housing of young people.

12 The right to veto unsuitable youth environments

In the cities, especially in Stockholm, there has been an important programme of investigating and of designating unsuitable youth environments. It is most important that local authorities should have the right of veto over the establishing of socially unsuitable enterprises.

We suggest that the local authorities are given planning control over leisure and cultural activities.

13 Culture commercialism

Much effort is required to oppose commercialism in the cultural field. The shaping of opinion is important. Youth organisations should be able to make a valuable contribution here.

We suggest a campaign against culture-commercialism. Youth organisations, on the basis of their own values should provide positive alternatives. We suggest that 1 per cent of tax revenue from advertising is redistributed to this campaign.

14 Intensified social support

Part of society's cultural provision should be in the form of support to various areas of culture — film, literature, the journal of organisations and cultural bodies, etc. There are discussions at present on subsidies for sound recording and art exhibitions.

We believe that the time is ripe for society to enhance those forms of support which aim to counteract the negative effects of commercialism. Society should make extra contributions to areas which have not yet been given support.

15 The need for a co-ordinated programme

A more co-ordinated programme must be drawn up, with measures for opposing culture-commercialism. This programme will require continued analysis of a complicated situation. The possibility of imposing further surcharges on cultural products in the commercial market should be investigated. Also, the circumstances of ownership and internationalisation in the cultural field should be studied further.

We suggest that bodies with cultural responsibility should plan a co-ordinated programme to oppose the negative effects of culture-commercialism.

The possibilities of financing increased cultural costs by means of surcharges of various kinds should be studied. Examples of products on which such surcharges could be imposed are: video-cassettes, video-discs, sound recordings, comics and magazines. A study should be made of circumstances of ownership and of internationalisation and the formation of cartels in various fields of the cultural industry.

16 Adult education

Adult education has always been central to the aims of the popular movements. Knowledge, the basis of opinion and involvement, is a human right. The study circle has long been the smallest element within adult education. This form of education must be safeguarded. It will be of even more importance in the future if our proposals for caring production are to be implemented. A forum for the exchange of experience will then be needed.

We believe that study circles and cultural activity within adult education are important for the skills of many people and, because of this, for the development of the local community.

17 Cultural institutions

Present day cultural centres — theatres, music institutions, museums, libraries, etc., reach a relatively small group of people. Many have a content which is of little interest to children and adolescents: they must develop their activities to reach new groups.

We believe that the cultural institutions must try to reach new groups in society and must be developed in order to reach areas which are today out of their range. They must adjust methods of working in order to reach children and adolescents.

18 Research and development in the cultural field

Developmental work in the cultural field is important, not least regarding research into cultural policy on children and adolescents. There is a great need for research which can form a basis for future planning.

We believe that there must be a guarantee of resources for a comprehensive programme of research, investigation and development in the field of cultural policy.

19 Social intervention

Society should not unnecessarily forbid or censor the commercial range of cultural activities. But, more and more frequently, it has appeared that manufacturers, with the stimulus of the profit motive, can produce almost any mutations they like. Society obviously has to set certain standards: so far, but no further. Intervention should be limited to the morality (or immorality) of the manufacturers.

We suggest that the enquiry into freedom of speech should consider a proposal for the previewing of video-recordings. There should be a further investigation into the bases for social intervention against mass-media merchandise which uses speculative violence, sexual discrimination and/or glorifies drugs.

20 Associations which serve the market

Many associations seem to be unaware of the strength of commercial youth culture, not least ideologically. The associations today are not the alternative to commercialism which might be desired. Direct links between many associations and commercial interests, especially in sport, in the form of advertisements and sponsorship, merit serious study.

We believe that those organisations which collaborate with commercial forces should plan to terminate this. Advertising deserves special attention.

21 Public support for the popular movements and associations

In times of austerity, cuts in public support to child and youth organisations are proposed. This would provide no real savings and could have serious social consequences.

We believe that savings in state and local authority grants to associations would have disastrous consequences, leading to increased social costs, among other things.

22 Age-integrated activities in associations

The popular movements ought to be in the forefront of co-operation between children and adults. One method would be to work more towards the integration of the activities of the old and young. Proposals of this kind should be given priority in relation to grant aid.

We suggest that, in future, support should be given to the popular movements for their age-integrated activities. Support should also be given for members over the age of 25, if children, adults and the elderly all work together.

23 The priority of children's organisations

Children must come into contact with association activities at an early age. This would be an aid to development, training children in the working methods of democracy. It also appears that those children who do not come into contact with associations at an early age do not become members when they grow older.

We suggest that children's and youth organisations should be given higher subsidies for their members up to the age of twelve, and that the lower age limit for subsidies to youth organisations are dispensed with.

24 The priority of affiliated associations

Today it is the affiliated associations which have the greatest difficulty in involving young people: the youth organisations of the traditional popular movements operate with great difficulties at local level. These affiliated associations ought to be given special subsidies.

We suggest that organisations for children and adolescents, which are affiliated to a certain philosophy, should be given greater aid compared to other child and youth organisations.

25 Imbalance in advertising

There is a deep imbalance between the collective resources of advertising (approx 6 billion kronor per year) and the commitments of consumer policy (approx 50 million kronor). It is especially important that consumer policy commitments geared towards children and adolescents are intensified.

We believe that the consumer policy commitment to children and adolescents should be increased. We suggest that 1 per cent of advertising revenue (the equivalent of ⅓ tax revenue from advertising) should be used to finance a campaign against the commercial youth culture, and that concrete proposals are worked out on the way in which the total gamut of advertising in our society can be reduced. A commission should be set up to examine the possibilities of imposing further surcharges on certain types of advertisements and on other methods of marketing products.

26 Advertising as product information

Information on the products' actual properties, prices, etc., are necessary if the consumers are to be able to make a free choice. Those advertisements which are emotional, non-factual and untrue should not be allowed.

We suggest that the legislation on marketing be supplemented so that unrelated pictures and texts, and also statements which cannot be substantiated, should not be allowed. Essentially one should only portray goods and describe their actual properties in advertisements.

27 Economic education

Children should be given another economic training than that which the commercial market represents. School and association activities should, to a greater extent, help children to analyse and discuss advertisements and compare various persuasion techniques.

We suggest that the government should change the composition of teacher training courses and of environmental studies and Swedish in comprehensive schools, introducing course elements on the analysis and identification of different persuasion techniques in marketing. This ought also to include the covert advertising which appears in newspapers, films, at discothèques, etc. Better conditions should be created to expand pupils' knowledge of marketing techniques and methods. The attractiveness of the commercial youth culture, in relation to the senses to which they appeal, should be the subject of discussion in school lessons. Journalists ought to intensify their own efforts at moderating the inadvertent amount of textual advertising.

173

28   Children and adolescents especially at risk

Developmental psychologists argue that children cannot distinguish between an advertisement's message and the truth. Advertising often exploits the child's need for imagination and idols. The amount of advertising to which children are exposed should be drastically reduced.

We suggest that legislation on marketing is amended, so that advertising and marketing aimed mainly at children under the age of 15 should not be allowed in direct advertising, in children's and adolescents' magazines and in the cinema.

29   Training in marketing

It is unacceptable that college courses in marketing should train their students in the most effective ways of manipulating the consumers. Their training must instead, and to a much greater extent, be in line with the aims of society's consumer policy.

We suggest that the government set the Higher Education Authority the task of changing the curricula for marketing courses in colleges, so that marketing itself will satisfy the consumers' needs of factual product information.

30   Advertising in the audio-visual media

It almost goes without saying that the media of television and radio in Sweden should still be kept free of advertising in future. This limitation on advertising ought to cover all present and future audio-visual media.

We suggest that the government ought to introduce a ban on advertising in audio-visual media, e.g. video plus any new broadcasting media which may be developed in the future.

A few facts . . .

. . . about today's young people

1   Today there are approximately 2.8 million young people under the age of 25 in Sweden. They make up 33 per cent of the country's population. Up to the year 2000, it is estimated that the number of young people under 25 will decrease to approximately 2.5 million. The relative proportion of young people in the population will also decrease.

2   Approximately 50 per cent of 18- to 24-year-olds say that they are interested in social questions. 64 per cent of students state that they have a great interest in social matters, as against 45 per cent of workers in employment.

3   Approximately 20 per cent of young people between 18 and 24 think that society is good as it is. 56 per cent think that it should be changed in some respect. 20 per cent believe that changes must be made in many areas. The least number of changes are desired by young working people, plus young people whose parents belong to the working class and young people with little interest in social questions.

4   31 per cent of young people between 15 and 18 have a clearly negative attitude to politics, 16 per cent are indifferent, 9 per cent are badly informed and 24 per cent abstain from answering. 21 per cent are clearly positive. Pupils on theoretical study programmes clearly have the greatest interest in politics.

5   In research among children of lower age-groups, it appears that Swedish children feel lonely to a greater extent than children in other countries being researched. Researchers compared children in Spain, Algeria, Israel, Ethiopia and Sweden. Children were allowed, *inter alia,* to react to the statement, 'I know that there is someone who likes me'. The children could choose between the responses 'often' 'sometimes' or 'never'. Most of the children in Sweden and abroad believe that they at least have *someone* who likes them. However, 11 per cent of Swedish children gave the response 'never'. In other countries, there do not appear to be any 'never-children'.

6   Girls (15 years olds) appear to have less self-confidence than boys. They worry more about their appearance, (a little over 50 per cent of girls as against 25 per cent of boys). 75 per cent of girls agree with the statement

* See Bibliography to Appendix 3 on pp 201–4

that they sometimes are of no use, as against 38 per cent of boys. Whilst 83 per cent of boys think they have many good characteristics, the equivalent percentage figure for girls is 60 per cent. 40 per cent of girls easily feel themselves failures, as against 17 per cent of boys.

7   84 per cent of young people in year group 9 (age 15–16) think it is important to take responsibility for others.

8   87 per cent of pupils in year group 9 think that meaningful work is the most essential thing for a rich, full life. 85 per cent think that the constant companionship of another person makes life richer. 81 per cent mention sport and other leisure occupations, 79 per cent state music, 69 per cent film and theatre, 66 per cent fantasy, 61 per cent books and publications and 59 per cent being a member of an association.

9   30 per cent of adolescents (15-year olds) believe that there are *no* advantages in becoming adult. Among the reasons for this are, first and foremost, not being disposed to having to work and take responsibility, and being worried at losing adult support and the freedom of childhood.
   The majority of 15-year-olds think, however, that becoming adult has its advantages. Above all they look forward to making their own decisions, doing as they wish and earning money.

10   Both boys and girls (10- to 12-year-olds) look forward to being able to work and earn money, approximately 26 per cent. Forming a family and having children appeal more to girls (15 per cent) than to boys (2 per cent).

. . . about child and adolescent consumption

11   As a rule, children's income in the form of, *inter alia,* pocket money, seasonal work, etc, rises more than average incomes in the country. During the period 1975 to 1977, young people's incomes rose by 17 per cent. They thus asserted well their economic position in relation to other groups in society.

12   In 1977 young people between 16 and 18 had command of a total of 1.6 billion kronor for their own consumption. The money principally went on clothes, beer, spirits, dancing, gramophone records, tobacco, haircare and the cinema.
   At the same time, young people owned capital goods for approx 3.5 billion kronor. The largest items were tape recorders, stereo systems, furniture, mopeds and other capital goods.

13   There are large differences between the sexes as regards consumption. Boys' ownership of capital goods in 70 per cent higher than girls. Boys own more, and above all, more expensive things than girls.

14   Young families with children (18–25 years) seem to struggle to retain their standards. Families with two or more children have an especially pressurised economy. The children's needs are served first; it seems important that one's own children do not have worse conditions than others — and a pressurised economy seems to have its greatest effect on the parents' standard.

15   The importance of consumer goods such as clothes and music seems to diminish in the upper age range (18–25 years). Expensive music systems and records are still bought but the importance of music in comparison with other interests seems to tail off.

16   78 per cent of young people (year groups 3, 5, 7 – ages 9, 11, 13) consider a bicycle to be the most necessary product. After that young people think that products used for listening to music are necessary (49 per cent).

17   Listening to music is an important part of young people's lives. Only 4 per cent of 15- to 18-year-olds are not especially interested in music. Of the collective value of those items owned by 15- to 18-year-olds, a tape recorder/stereo lies in first place in the survey (1977) at 750 billion kronor.

18   79 per cent of young people think that making purchases is fun. This positive attitude increases with age.

19   Most young people say that they prefer buying a new, more expensive capital item rather than a cheaper secondhand one. The disinclination to buy secondhand increases with age.

20   Half the adolescents prefer to wait to buy jeans until they can afford to buy the *right* ones, rather than buying a pair of cheap ones on economic grounds.

21   Young people become, with age, more dependent on the opinions of their friends and less dependent on those of their parents.

22   61 per cent of girls from social group 3 make their purchases principally in department stores as against 10 per cent of girls from social group 1.

23   94 per cent of girls in social group 3 say they are very or quite interested in clothes, as against 79 per cent of girls from social group 1.

24   73 per cent of girls in social group 1 say they have their own style of dressing as against 22 per cent of girls from social group 3.

25   61 per cent girls from social group 3 think that it is fun to go around and look at furniture, as against 31 per cent of girls from social group 1.

26   46 per cent from social group 1 spend part of their holiday in their own summer cottage as against 14 per cent of girls from social group 3.

27   45 per cent of girls from social group 3 go camping during their holidays as against 2 per cent of girls from social group 1.

28   59 per cent of young people between 15 and 24 believe that advertising encourages unnecessary consumption, only 8 per cent believe that it does not do so. 49 per cent think that it would be good if there were fewer advertisements. Only 3 per cent think that advertisements give the product information which the consumer needs. 64 per cent think that advertising ought to represent impartial consumer information to a greater extent. 63 per cent of young people between 15 and 24 wish to completely ban advertisements which are directed at children.

29   56 per cent (year groups 3, 5, 7) think it is a good thing that there are advertisements. 58 per cent are positive to the extent that they think advertisements are fun. At the same time, 89 per cent think that what is stated in advertisements is exaggerated. 51 per cent think that advertisements for sweets are wrong.

30   Despite the fact that direct advertising to children is limited, so far, and despite the fact that the major proportion of direct advertising deals with goods which young people do not buy themselves, approximately 30 per cent of them, nevertheless, read the advertisements which come through the letterbox (year groups 3, 5, 7).

31   77 per cent of young people believe that advertisements which portray woman as inferior to men ought to be banned.

32   30 per cent of those between 15 and 24 want to have advertising on television, as against 24 per cent of the total population. The older the children are the more positive is their attitude to advertising on television.

33   Just over half of adolescents think it is very important that schools provide consumer information. Only 4 per cent believe that it is unimportant.

34   78 per cent of the Swedish teachers in comprehensive schools make use of various forms of commercial material in their lessons. It is most common among teachers in the cities.

35   97 per cent of households with children have television. 74 per cent have colour television. 75 per cent of households with children have more than one television.

36   81 per cent of households with children have stereo systems as against 51 per cent overall. 77 per cent of 9- to 14-year-olds have access to a stereo and 84 per cent of 18- to 24-years-olds.

37   88 per cent of households with children have at least one record, 10 per cent have up to 20.

38   59 per cent of 9- to 14-year-olds and 41 per cent of 15- to 24-year-olds do not normally read a daily newspaper. The equivalent figure for the population as a whole is 26 per cent. 72 per cent of 9- to 14-year-olds and 53 per cent of 15- to 24-year-olds do not normally read an evening paper, as against 61 per cent of the population as a whole.

39   The *Pressbyrån* chain of newsagents sells 34 million comics for 123 million kronor each year.

40   Just over 25 per cent of 11-year-olds carry out some task for which they get paid. 33 per cent intend to obtain some occupation for which they will get paid.

41   75 per cent of 16-year-olds have or have had some form of work which provides them with money. 70 per cent of boys and 60 per cent of girls worked for varying lengths of time during the last summer vacation.

42   90 per cent of parents of 16-year-olds believe that it is correct for their son/daughter of this age to have a little extra work.

43   Most 11-year-olds have weekly or monthly pocket money. 25 per cent get, in addition, extra money if they have to do something special or if they are to buy something special.

44   Approximately 33 per cent of 16-year-olds spend 20 to 39 kronor per week. 20 per cent spend 40 to 59 kronor per week and 20 per cent have 60 kronor or more to spend for their own consumption.

45   90 per cent of 11-year-olds think they have just the right amount of money to spend. Boys are more dissatisfied than girls, however. 70 per cent of 16-year-olds are materially satisfied.

46   95 per cent of the parents of 11-year-olds and 90 per cent of parents of 16-year-olds believe that their children have just the right amount of money at their disposal.

47   In certain cases, especially among parents in social group 3, parents think that their 16-year-olds have too little money at their command. This is said by as many as 20 per cent in social group 3, as against 4 per cent in social group 1.

48   Single parents say, twice as often as co-habiting/married parents, that adolescents have too little money at their command.

49   Only 4 per cent of 11-year-olds think that the most enjoyable thing to do after school is to play with their possessions. 40 per cent of boys think that taking part in sport is the most enjoyable. Girls think, instead, that the most enjoyable thing is spending time with their friends.

50   Children often want to have pets. 68 per cent of 11-year-olds have access to pets at home. It is, most of all, girls who want to have pets, 22 per cent.

51   50 per cent of girls and 75 per cent of boys intend to procure a car in a few years' time. 20 per cent of girls as opposed to only 7 per cent of boys intend to get a flat.

52   In a 'normal' day, 11-year-olds mostly buy sweets and soft drinks. Most 11-year-olds spend a sum of 5 kronor or less per week on confec-

tionery and sweets. Those who spend most money on sweets are children from flats. They differ in this connection from children from villas.

53   17 per cent of 16-year-olds *went shopping* for half an hour or more 'yesterday', that is, on a normal weekday. Just over 50 per cent bought *something* 'yesterday'.

54   77 per cent of boys and 67 per cent of girls watched television for half an hour or more 'yesterday evening'.

55   More than 50 per cent of girls as against approximately 30 per cent of boys would like more dance venues and discothèques.

56   More than 70 per cent of 16-year-olds generally think that they have just the right number of clothes.

57   Half of all boys say they do not know what is the latest fashion in clothes. Only 16 per cent of girls suffer from the same 'ignorance'.

58   However, most young people know what is 'in'. 58 per cent of girls as opposed to 25 per cent of boys also intend to get themselves whatever is 'in'.

59   More than half of the parents of 11-year-olds say they do not think that fashion has really changed in the past few years, neither for better nor worse. 85 per cent of the parents offer no set criticism of the fashions of today.

60   It is more usual for parents within social group 3 to say that young people spend too little money on clothes rather than too much (10 per cent as against 3 per cent).

61   27 per cent of those parents of 11-year-olds who live in villas state that they themselves have to cut down on their clothes so that their children are able to get what they want and need. The equivalent figure for parents living in flats is 12 per cent.

62   The adolescents (16-year-olds) who went dancing most, are to be found among those who live in flats. Young people who live in villas/terraced housing go out dancing more seldom.

63   Half of the boys and 30 per cent of the girls say they they never or hardly ever go dancing.

64   Half of the adolescents (aged 16) were abroad in the summer before they went into yeargroup 9. Above all it was young people from social group 1 who travelled abroad.

65   Only 3 per cent of boys and 1 per cent of girls (aged 16) have travelled with the Interail pass.

66   23 per cent of adolescents from social group 1 were on a charter trip, as against 8 per cent of those from social group 3.

67   Going to camp is primarily a summer activity of young people from social group 1, 36 per cent in social group 1 as against 21 per cent in social group 3.

68   35 per cent of young people say that on the whole they want to have the same or similar clothes as their friends.

69   More than 80 per cent of 11-year-olds believe their parents have just enough say in the matter of buying clothes.

70   44 per cent of parents of 16-year-olds say they influence their children's choice of clothing. Among 11-year-olds it is only 7 per cent who themselves decide, in detail, what should be bought. Among 16-year-olds it is 35 per cent.

. . . about school

71   In the school year 1979 to 1980, a total of 1,043,000 pupils went to local authority comprehensive schools.

72   Immigrant pupils, with a language other than Swedish spoken at home, made up 8.2 per cent of all comprehensive school pupils in the autumn of 1979. 47 per cent of the immigrants speak Finnish at home. After those come pupils with Yugoslavian (8.7 per cent), German (7.3 per cent), Danish (5.2 per cent), Spanish (3.9 per cent) and English (3.4 per cent) as their mother tongue.

73   41 per cent of 15-year-old city-girls as against 37 per cent of boys are positive towards school. Around 30 per cent have a negative attitude.

74   If the pupils were allowed to be 'headmaster for a day', 50 per cent of the boys and 33 per cent of the girls would, to a great extent, leave things as they are. 40 per cent of girls as against 49 per cent of boys would allow smoking.

75   The results of standard tests in school greatly corresponds with the social grouping of the pupils. The higher the social group, the better the results. The more pupils from social group 3 within a class (low status classes), the worse the results were for all pupils and vice versa.

76   Teachers have better contact with parents from social group 1 (11.3 per cent positive, 0.9 per cent negative, 0.2 per cent negligible) compared with social group 3 parents (7.9 per cent positive, 1.6 per cent negative and 8.5 per cent negligible).

77   Choice of study programme at sixth form college is still very closely linked with the sexes of the pupils. For girls the dominant subjects are: 2-year consumer studies course (97.7 per cent), 2-year clothing course (97.4 per cent) 2-year nursing studies course (94 per cent) and 2-year distribution

and office studies course (80.4 per cent). Boy-dominated subjects are: 2-year technical (engineering) course (98.7 per cent), 2–year technical (building and construction) (98.3 per cent), 2-year technical (electrical) (98.3 per cent). In addition, girls are in the majority in the 3-year arts and social sciences study programmes (approximately 75 per cent) while boys dominate the 3-year sciences study programme (56 per cent) and the 4-year technical study programme (88.5 per cent).

78   95 per cent of children of academics go on from comprehensive school to sixth-form college. Among children of workers without professional training 67 per cent go on to sixth-form education.

79   26 per cent of boys and 24 per cent of girls begin work after compre-hensive school. 76 per cent of boys and 74 per cent of girls begin sixth-form education. 17 per cent of boys and 22 per cent of girls begin higher education.

. . . about children, adolescents, families and housing/care

80   At 31 December 1979 Sweden had a population of approximately 8.3 million. Of these 42 per cent were married. Just over 2 million were young people aged between 7 and 24 and 1.3 million were elderly, aged 65 and over.

81   The number of young people in the population is decreasing consis-tently with the increase in numbers of the elderly.

82   The size of households has steadily decreased. In 1920, the average household consisted of 4.3 people, in 1930 of 3.5 people and in 1975 of 2.4 people.

83   30 per cent of households consist of single people
      26 per cent of two co-habiting adults with children
      27 per cent of two co-habiting adults with no children
       9 per cent of one adult with children.

84   81.4 of those men who got married in 1979 were over 25. Only 0.6 per cent were under 20. Women get married at an earlier age than men.

85   88 per cent of all 16- to 19-year-olds who are living together are not married. 61 per cent of 20- to 24-year-olds are not married.

86   Approximately half of the population is unmarried. However, approximately 90 per cent of the population will get married at some time in their lives.

87   The frequency of divorces is rising — this is an international pheno-menon, as is the increase in unmarried couples living together. In 1935, 1 per cent of the age group 30 to 34 were divorced, as against 7 per cent of

men and 9 per cent of women approximately 30 years later. In 1966, 10,000 divorces were carried out whereas almost twice that number, that is, just over 20,000, were carried out in 1978. Of the marriages solemnised in 1971, 8 per cent were dissolved four years later. For co-habiting relationships the equivalent figure was 18 per cent. About half of all marriages will be dissolved in the long term.

88   The frequency of gainful employment remains constant for men, but is still rising for women. In an historical perspective, the picture has been radically altered for women. In 1930, 9 per cent of married women were gainfully employed; in 1945 — 11 per cent; in 1950 — 15 per cent; in 1960 — 26 per cent; in 1970 — 55 per cent and in 1979 — 70 per cent.
    Among unmarried women the frequency rose from 59 per cent in 1930 to 72 per cent in 1977. However, a very large proportion of women are in part-time employment.

89   In the present generation of children, probably less than 10 per cent will have a 'housewife' mother for the whole period of their growing up.

90   At the turn of the year 1978/79, 45.7 per cent of all children aged between 0 to 6 years had parents who were both gainfully employed or studying. Only 15 per cent of the children had places in day nurseries, however. In addition to these, 10.3 per cent had places in family day nurseries.

91   55 per cent of children aged between 3 and 8 are cared for by their mothers during the daytime, 1 per cent by their fathers, 6 per cent alternately by mother/father; 10 per cent are looked after by a child minder/mother's help; a further 10 per cent by child minder/parent; 8 per cent by day nurseries/parent and 9 per cent by day nursery/play school.

92   17 per cent of 3- to 8-year-olds have mothers who work full-time; 38 per cent have mothers working part-time; 4 per cent of mothers are students and 40 per cent work in the home. Up to 89 per cent of fathers work full-time and 2 per cent part-time; 1 per cent are students and 0 per cent work in the home.

93   Among children of parents with little education, 49 per cent have mothers working in the home, as against 27 per cent of highly educated parents. 11 per cent of children of parents with little education have places at day nurseries, 15 per cent of children of parents with average education and 24 per cent of children of highly educated parents.

94   A large proportion of city-adolescents are positively disposed to eventually living with someone. Approximately 50 per cent are for marriage. Young people from social group 1 and 2 are more positive towards marriage than those from social group 3.

95   99 per cent of adolescents (year group 9) think that it is important to 'get on with and have fun together with' their future partner. Faithfulness

is also rated highly (97 per cent). 74 per cent answer that having interests in common means quite a lot or a lot.

96   72 per cent of boys place importance on the fact that their partner is good-looking as opposed to 36 per cent of girls. Boys are more particular that their partner has had no previous sexual relationships — 14 per cent, as against 4 per cent of girls.

97   46 per cent of boys (15–16 and 18-year-olds) think that sex, appearance and clothes are important characteristics for a girl, 18 per cent of girls think that they are important in boys. Furthermore, both sexes were quite in agreement that behaviour, kindness, openness, intelligence and sense of humour are important traits in their partners.

98   Between 65 per cent and 90 per cent of 15- to 18-year-olds consider that they feel 'affection for their parents and that these feel affection for them'. Boys feel most affection and greatest interest from their mothers. Girls, too, have closer relations with their mothers than their fathers.

99   Just over 50 per cent of 15-year-old boys say that they often talk to their mothers. Only 39 per cent of girls say that they often talk to their fathers, while boys talk equally as often to both parents.

100   Companionship with brothers and sisters does not seem to hold a prominent position in the lives of adolescents. Between 46 per cent and 60 per cent of 15- to 18-year-olds state that they spend very little, or little time with their brothers and sisters.

101   62 per cent of 18-year-olds boys and 39 per cent of girls in the city surveys were of the opinion that *no adult apart from their parents* had had any great significance for them during their childhood. 25 per cent of girls believed that their maternal grandparents had been of importance as against only 8 per cent of boys. Even fewer, only 4 per cent of adolescents, credit their paternal grandparents with any significance.

102   To the question on which person meant most to 18-year-olds, 32 per cent of girls now answer, in the first instance, 'my boyfriend'. Only 14 per cent of boys answer 'my girlfriend'. The highest percentage figure of boys was given to the response alternative of 'nobody special'.

103   In the 15–16 age group, 61 per cent of girls have a best friend. A few years later the proportion has sunk to approximately 35 per cent. The equivalent proportions for boys are 25 per cent and 14 per cent.

104   The girls' circle of friends is often smaller than the boys'. 24 per cent of boys had 5 friends or more as against 9 per cent of girls.

105   43 per cent of girls in a city survey worry about not being popular among their friends as against 25 per cent of boys. Nearly all girls think that a girlfriend means a lot to them (98 per cent). For boys the equivalent figure is 86 per cent.

106   In 1975 there were 16,979 young people between the ages of 16 and 29 who were prematurely retired/on invalidity benefit. In 1979, the figure was 16,089.

107   In 1963, 74 boys and 39 girls committed suicide. The equivalent figures for 1978 were 114 and 44 respectively.

108   Approximately 50 per cent of schoolchildren have their own room. 67 per cent in social groups 1 and 2 have their own room as against 33 per cent of children in social group 3.

. . . about children, adolescents, drugs and criminality

109   The number of intoxicated persons taken into custody, aged under 14, were: in 1975, 383; in 1979, 386. In the age group 15–17, the figures were: in 1975, 4458 and in 1979, 3285. In the age group 18–19, 5930 people were taken into custody in 1975 as against 5230 in 1979.

110   Today the number of registered crimes committed by 15- to 17-year-olds is fifteen times greater than the equivalent for 1920.

111   Just over 40 per cent of all vandalism is perpetrated by young people under 25. Just over 25 per cent of all fraud is committed by young people.

112   It is mostly boys who commit crime. It is calculated that approximately 80 per cent of all crime in Sweden is committed by men. Teenagers seldom commit crime alone. It is almost always a question of a group, a gang of the same age group.

113   The social welfare authorities' resolutions on preventive measures because of parental problems has increased greatly during the 1970s, from approximately 1000 children per year in 1971, to more than 2600 children in 1978. On the other hand, the social welfare authorities' resolutions on problem children in care, have decreased quite markedly during the 1970s.

114   Consumption of alcohol is widespread even among younger adolescents. Among 13- to 16-year-olds, 76 per cent already drink alcohol at some time during a one-year period. 12 per cent of these drink alcohol once a week or more frequently. Among 16-year-olds, 27 per cent drink once a week or more frequently.

115   The numbers of those who never drink alcohol vary in different age groups: 13-year-olds, 39 per cent; 14-year-olds, 17 per cent; 15-year-olds, 10 per cent; 16-year-olds, 9 per cent; 17-year-olds, 10 per cent; 18- to 19-year-olds, 5 per cent.

116   Among 17- to 19-year-olds, 93 per cent drink alcohol, 15 per cent drink every week, 60 per cent a least once a month.

117   Girls in the age group 13–16 drink alcohol just as often as boys.

118   Alcohol consumption in litres/year: 13 years 1.25 litres; 14 years 2.51 litres; 15 years 3.71 litres; 16 years; 6.54 litres; 17 years 2.41 litres; 18 years 3.51 litres; 19 years 3.57 litres; 20–29 years 2.86 litres; 30–74 years approximately 2 litres.

119   40 per cent of 13-year-olds state that they first drank alcohol before the age of twelve.

120   Among 13- to 16-year-olds there is a clear connection between the alcohol consumption of parents and adolescents. If parents do not use alcohol their children as a rule also refrain (57 per cent). If parents drink often then only 9 per cent of their children refrain from alcohol.

121   Of the 13- to 16-year-olds who use alcohol, 50 per cent state that they sometimes drink with their parents. 71 per cent of 13- to 16-year-olds have at some time been offered alcohol by their parents. Among 17- to 19-year-olds the equivalent figure is 79 per cent.

122   Amongst those in the age group 13–16 who drink alcohol, parents have in a third of the cases procured a certain proportion of the alcohol which the adolescents have drunk during the past year. The category of suppliers who are of the greatest significance, next to parents, are friends.

123   In 1971, 68 per cent of boys and 60 per cent of girls in year group 6, stated that they drank alcohol. In 1979, the proportion had dropped to 60 per cent and 49 per cent respectively. Amongst boys in year group 9, 91 per cent stated that they drank alcohol as against 86 per cent in 1979. The figure for girls remains unchanged at 90 per cent.

124   Among boys in year group 9, 14 per cent had at some time tried out drugs, in 1971. In 1979, the proportion had dropped to 7 per cent. Of girls in year group 9, 17 per cent had taken drugs at some time, in 1971. In 1979, the figure was down to 6 per cent. 2 per cent of boys and 1 per cent of girls in year group 9 continue to take drugs (more or less regularly) in 1979.

125   Solvent sniffing has decreased during the 1970s. In 1972 94 per cent of boys and 96 per cent of girls in year group 6 stated that they had never sniffed solvents. In 1979 these figures had gone up to 98 per cent and 99 per cent respectively. In 1972 the figures for year group 9 were 80 per cent for boys and 85 per cent for girls. In 1979 the proportion of those who had never sniffed solvents had risen to 95 per cent and 96 per cent respectively. Only 1 to 2 per cent of all pupils in both year groups state, in 1979, that they are solvent sniffers.

126   Smoking, too, is on the decrease among young people. In 1971, 14 per cent of boys and 16 per cent of girls in year group 6 smoked. In 1979 the figures had gone down to 6 per cent and 8 per cent respectively. There is also a marked decrease among pupils in year group 9. There are only half as many boy smokers in 1979 (21 per cent), compared with 1971 (41 per cent). Among girls the drop is not quite so large. In 1971, 47 per cent were smokers and in 1979, 34 per cent.

. . . about children, adolescents and work

127 Of all unemployed people in Sweden, in January 1981, 38 per cent were young people under 25. In January 1981, 10,128 young people took part in government-sponsored work schemes, that being 16,087 fewer than in the previous year. This can be traced back to the change in regulations for government-sponsored work schemes. 13,700 young people under 25 took part in training for the employment market in January 1981.

128 The figures for youth unemployment for January 1980 and January 1981 show that it is mostly women between the ages of 16 and 19 who are hit by rising unemployment.

129 Young people between 16 and 19 are, when they get work, more vulnerable to physical strain than other age groups. They are also to the greatest extent employed in dirty employment. 44 per cent of young people thought that their work was stressful; 31 per cent that it was monotonous and 36 per cent believed that they did not have enough influence over the planning of their work.

130 In 1979 the proportion of people in the age group 16–24 in the total workforce was an average of 71 per cent. For foreign citizens in Sweden the figure was 77.8 per cent. In the same year, 1979, 7.7 per cent of all young people aged between 16 and 19 were unemployed. For foreign adolescents of the same ages, in Sweden, the figure was 10.7 per cent.

. . . about children and adolescents, leisure and mass-media consumption

131 Watching television, listening to music and reading comics are highest in the list, in all surveys, of what children and adolescents do in their free-time.

132 Many young people also spend their free-time outside the home, together with their friends, in what can collectively be called non-organised activities. Among these as the commercial alternatives available. Of 13- to 24-year-olds in Stockholm more than 90 per cent have been to the cinema at some time during the previous three-month period; 40 per cent go as often as at least once every other week. Visits to pubs or hamburger bars are also common. Just over 80 per cent of young people have visited such premises periodically, and 25 per cent do so once or many times per week.

133 A comprehensive school pupil spends between 15 and 30 hours per week in front of the TV, which is equivalent to 22–45 school periods. A normal school week contains approximately 35 periods. Calculated as annual consumption of TV this means that Swedish school pupils, from year group 1 up to the sixth form, sit for a greater number of hours in their TV-chairs than at their school desks.

134   Within each year group there are super-consumers of television, who look at a total of 12 hours just on Saturdays, equivalent to 18 school periods in *one* day.

135   80 per cent of parents believe that their 11-year-olds look at good television programmes.

136   Saturday is, above all other days, the children's TV-day; 37 per cent look at more than 3 hours of television on Saturday evening, 3- to 8-year-olds watch an average of 170 minutes.

137   On Saturdays, 9 per cent of 3- to 8-year-olds watch television until 8.30 pm; 38 per cent continue to watch until 9.30 pm and 4 per cent are still watching television even later than that.

138   18 per cent (100,000 children) in the age group 3 to 8, usually fall asleep in front of the television at least once a week or more frequently.

139   Before 6.30 pm, 65 per cent of children in the age group 3 to 8, watch programmes alone. Among 9- to 14-year-olds the figure is 69 per cent.

140   67 per cent of parents of children in the age group 3 to 8, state that their children have become frightened during some television programme. Half of the programmes which are stated as being frightening are children and family programmes.

141   28 per cent of 9- to 14-year-olds go dancing at least once a week and 30 per cent of 15- to 24-year-olds as against 16 per cent of the total population.

142   58 per cent of all cinema visits are made by young people aged between 15 and 24. Of these 64 per cent are boys and 36 per cent girls.

143   Nine out of ten pupils in comprehensive schools read comics. When the children get older, weekly magazine reading takes over. *Fantomen* (*The Phantom*) is the most popular magazine among 15- to 19-year-olds. Among 20- to 24-year-olds, *FIB—Aktuellt* (*Topical People in Pictures*) is the most popular amongst boys and *Damernas Värld* (*Ladies World*) amongst girls.

144   32 per cent of 9- to 14-year-olds read books for at least half an hour during an average day. For 15- to 24-year-olds the proportion is 27 per cent. The average percentage figures for the whole population is 21 per cent.

. . . about children, adolescents and associations

145   There are 39,350 local youth associations, with 4 million members between the ages of 0 to 25; 440,000 association leaders; 1500 full time employees in Sweden today.

146   Youth associations have a turnover of approximately 600 million kronor per year.

147   Approximately 60 per cent of all young people aged between 10 and 12 are members of some association. However, differences between the sexes do start to enter into the picture as the children grow older. Girl membership drops dramatically. At the age of 15, 58 per cent of girls are in an association, 50 per cent at 16 and 44 per cent at 18. Boys, on the other hand, remain at around 60 per cent or just over. There are also differences between social groups. In social group 1, two thirds of the adolescents are members of an association, as against only half of those in social group 3. Closely related to social grouping is the type of school education. The proportion of those affiliated to associations is especially high among young people with a more theoretically oriented education. It is especially low among girls in paid employment; of these, only 35 per cent are members of any organisation.

148   In an investigation carried out in Stockholm, in 1979, among young people between the ages of 13 and 20, it was also shown that just over 60 per cent of these are members of an association. Boys are affiliated to associations to a greater extent than girls, here, too. This is especially so among older ones, that is to say that girls' involvement in associations decreases the older they become. Areas which are male-dominated are almost exclusively within sport and outdoor organisations.

149   Two thirds of all boys who are members of an association are members of a sports association, as against half of the girls. Membership of religious associations is, however, more common among girls. The proportion of those in temperance associations drops dramatically with age. Of 18-year-olds, only 1 per cent are members. The opposite is true of political associations where the proportion rises from 2 per cent to 6 per cent between the ages of 15 and 18. The remaining associations, that is associations for hobbies and interests such as music, photography, automobiles, stamps, etc, attract many members, 15 per cent of both boys and girls.

150   Members of associations spend a great deal of time on their association work. The average is 6 hours per week.

151   According to the youth survey of SIFO (Swedish National Institute for Opinion Research) in 1979/80, 22 per cent of young people aged between 16 and 19 and 52 per cent of young people aged between 20 and 24 are members of a trades union; 8 per cent and 9 per cent, respectively, are members of a political youth organisation; 5 per cent in both age groups are members of non-conformist church associations and 1 per cent are members of another church association; 1 per cent of both age groups are members of temperance associations; 45 per cent of those aged 16–19 and 39 per cent of those aged 20–24, are members of a sports association. Singing and music associations attract 7 per cent and 5 per cent

189

respectively, of young people in both age groups. Automobile associations attract just as many. Other types of associations involve 14 per cent of 16–19-year-olds and 17 per cent of 20–24-year-olds.

152 In a survey in Malmö, great differences between residential areas were brought to light, regarding pupils' involvement in associations. The lowest association membership figures were in some of the more recent housing developments in the district, while areas with villas and terraced housing generally had larger association memberships than areas with blocks of flats.

153 In a survey of the working conditions for local associations which was carried out by the Youth Council in 1979, it apears that an association has, on average, approximately 60 members. The number of leaders per association is 6 on average. 83 per cent of associations do not have any employed officials, all work being done on a voluntary basis by members. An average of 15,000 kronor/year is spent by each association on their child and youth activities. Society contributes towards half of the running costs of child and youth activities; a state subsidy of 11 per cent, a local authority subsidy of 38 per cent, a regional authority subsidy of 1 per cent, membership fees provide 5 per cent and other sources (bingo, bazaars, lotteries, etc) provide 45 per cent.

154 The form of education is decisive for becoming a member of an association. The numbers of those in associations are especially high among young people with a more theoretically oriented education, compared with young people on a more practical study programme or who are in employment. 75 per cent of all boys in theoretically oriented education are members of an association while 35 per cent of the employed girls are members (true for young people of 18 years of age).

155 Young people state that they have relatively little interest in politics and social matters but that, at the same time, they believe it is important to be involved in political questions. This is where the differences between different groups of young people are represented most clearly. 38 per cent of pupils on theoretical study programmes at school are positive towards politics. The equivalent figure for young people in employment is 11 per cent. In figures for young people from social group 1 on theoretical study programmes and for unemployed youngsters are compared, the differences become even more marked, 45 per cent as against 3 per cent. Two reasons above all for the low level of interest are given by the young people; a generally low opinion of politics, and a lack of knowledge. Young people believe that politics are difficult but that they generally (approximately 50 per cent) wish to learn more about political matters.

156 Even at the age of 12—and in any case 15—the associations have reached all of those who will ever be reached. After this age, one only changes association or joins even more associations.

157 Sports associations have the greatest membership (approximately 60 per cent of all members are in some sports association). In addition, the proportion of those who are members in 'other youth organisations', i.e. leisure and hobby associations, appears to increase steadily. Their proportion of membership is now equal to that of the sports organisations. The increase of the group 'other associations' seems to happen at the cost of the sports organisations.

158 The religious associations have approximately 4 per cent as members. Temperance associations have approximately 1 per cent as members. 5 per cent are members of political associations. Thus, the so-called ideologically affiliated associations are struggling with considerable odds when it comes to reaching young people.

159 Local associations generally have approximately 60 children affiliated to them; sports associations have quite a varied composition of ages, while for example, the Scouts, *Unga Örnar* (*Young Eagles*) and *Förbundet Vi Unga* (*The League of Youth*) generally have most members in the age group 7–12. 80 per cent of the religious associations have most of their membership in as low an age group as the 0–12-year-olds.

160 The number of leaders in local associations is 6 on average. Only every sixth association has an employed member of staff. It is, above all, within sports associations and within the religious associations that there are employed leaders.

161 Society takes responsibility for half of the associations' costs for child and youth activities; state subsidy for 11 per cent; local authority subsidy for 38 per cent and regional authority subsidy for 1 per cent. The remaining half is financed by the associations themselves.

162 Many associations experience competition from other directions. The greatest problem is competition from other associations, above all sports associations. Sports associations also see competition from other sports associations as their greatest problem. The associations say the least competition comes from private discotheques, dances, cinemas, amusement arcades, etc, whereas local authority competition is seen as a little greater. The political associations and temperance associations believe that private competition is greater than that of the local authority.

163 It seems that many associations are on their way to a four-day week. Approximately half of them believe that Friday/Saturday/Sunday are difficult days on which to run their activities.

164 Television is a great competitor for many associations. Others, e.g. sports associations, are rather more positive towards television, since television advertises their activities. The religious associations, especially, see television as encouraging passivity.

165 Among the most important obstacles to developing their activities,

the associations name the shortage of leaders as the one most dominating; following this are economic obstacles and lack of premises.

166 The most important problems for associations today are leaders, finance and premises.

Within sports associations it is the shortage of leaders and premises which is most acute. The sports associations hardly ever mention young people's lack of interest, of difficulties in keeping members, as any problem. The Scouts, *Unga Örnar* and *Förbundet Vi Unga* also mention shortage of leaders. Within religious associations the shortage of leaders is great, but shortage of money is hardly ever mentioned.

Political associations mention shortage of leaders relatively seldom, but the overshadowing problem which stands out is the youngsters' lack of interest in the activities.

167 Association leaders are often afraid that in future it will become difficult to involve leaders on a voluntary basis. They see themselves as 'the last of the madmen'.

168 The association leaders often believe that they have an educational role in society. The most important element of this is that they feel responsible for passing on society's values to young people. The association leaders often feel that they cope with their educational role rather better than, for example, institutions such as schools do.

169 The association leaders are often proud of the history of their associations. Events from the day-to-day activities of association work are often transmitted orally to others.

170 Today's association leaders seem to experience a dual role of both being part of the established social system and being outside it.

171 Most associations have a negative view of their development over the past ten years. The voluntary ideal has diminished—it is more difficult to recruit leaders, and competition has increased. The most negative are the Scouts, *Unga Örnar,* and *Förbundet Vi Unga,* the temperance associations and the political associations.

172 Most associations (who submitted responses) believe that it will become increasingly difficult in future. The voluntary element will diminish further, competition will increase.

173 70 per cent of 11-year-olds today are members of some association; boys somewhat more frequently than girls. These figures indicate a rise of at least 10 per cent since 1972. The reason might be that the age limit for subsidies was dropped from 12 to 7 years of age.

174 It is somewhat more common for those from social group 1 to be members than those from social group 3. The most common form of membership among 11-year-olds is sport, and young people from social group 3 are recruited somewhat more frequently into these. The Scouts,

Unga Örnar and *Vi Unga,* that is, to a large extent the children's organisations, have in percentage terms twice as many 11-year-olds from social group 1, as from social group 3. Other organisations also have their greatest support from social group 1. Religious and temperance organisations have very few members in Helsingborg and rather more in Skellefteå; 0 per cent as against 7 per cent for temperance organisations and 1 per cent as against 18 per cent for the religious organisations.

175   62 per cent of 16-year-olds are members of some association. Approximately 33 per cent state that they are not members. The rest have not answered the question, which might really be interpreted as meaning that they are not members of any association; thus the proportion of those not members of associations can be estimated at approximately 38 per cent. The figures agree well with our earlier surveys in 1972 and 1974.

176   The differences between the sexes are still great, most of all because sports associations recruit so many more boys than girls. 59 per cent of boys are in some sports association, as against only 23 per cent of girls.

Differences between social groups are small, however, with regard to sports associations, even if rather more are recruited from social group 1. Different sports vary quite a lot in this respect. Within football organisations, for example, social group 3 is in the majority instead.

177   Among 16-year-olds, the Scouts, *Unga Örnar* and *Vi Unga* have a relatively even distribution, regarding sex and social group. We can compare this to the situation among 11-year-olds. The percentage decrease among children from social group 1 can perhaps be interpreted as that these children are very active in a number of enterprises and organisations and therefore leave these organisations to a greater extent than do children from social group 3.

There are very few members of temperance organisations among 16-year-olds. The religious associations recruit three times as frequently from social group 1 as from social group 3, 12 per cent as against 4 per cent.

178   The political youth organisations attract just over 4 per cent of young people. In this case, it is five times as common to be a member if one comes from social group 1 compared with those coming from social group 3; 10 per cent as against 2 per cent.

The proportion is 10:1 as regards people from social group 1 living in villas compared to those from social group 3 who live in flats. It is also ten times as common to become a member of a political association if one comes from social group 1 and lives in a villa compared to those coming from social group 3 living in flats.

179   Many boys are members of more than one association. A tenth of boys are leaders of some association. Interest in going on a leadership training course is greater among girls, 35 per cent as against 16 per cent. It is more usual to be interested in becoming a leader in social group 3. There

is therefore a large unexploited reserve of leaders. Associations ought perhaps to increase their efforts to recruit leaders in this group, especially if, as we have shown, leaders are now primarily recruited from social groups 1 and 2.

180   What are the costs of association membership and leisure interests? We put the question as to whether 16-year-olds have any special interest or any special hobby, on which they spend a lot or quite a lot of money. Not unexpectedly, a majority of them did have; more boys than girls. Only 22 per cent of boys said that they did not spend a lot, or quite a lot, of money on any special interest or any special hobby, as against 42 per cent of girls. For girls, horse-riding costs most; for boys, it is football or some other sport. 35 per cent of the boys say that they spend a lot, or quite a lot, of money on their sporting interest, whereas 19 per cent of the girls said so.

181   11-year-olds have massive support, at least economically, from their parents, regarding their hobby activities and other leisure interests. Almost three-quarters of the parents contribute money or presents to their 11-year-olds' various leisure interests. Support is strongest among parents of boys and among parents in social group 1. It is usually parents living in flats and coming from social group 3 who say that they do not, for various reasons, economically support the leisure interests of their children. This may be for purely economic reasons, or because the children do not have such high economic demands, or interests which cost especially large amounts of money.

182   The parents of 11-year-olds are especially positive towards sports organisations. Their strong position among children and young people is therefore echoed in the parental group. Almost 30 per cent say that they would like their 11-year-olds to be involved in sport. But there is also a large group of parents, 55 per cent, who do not respond to the question as to whether they would like their children to be involved in any special association.

Notes

References below are expanded in the Bibliography on pp 197–200.

Chapter 1

1 ETS* pp 55–59, 261–262.
  Ladurie, 1980
2 Dale, 1981
3 ETS p 265
4 Hanssen, 1978
5 ETS p 262–265
  Liljeström *et al* 1979
6 Liljeström 1981
7 ETS p 57
8 Bjurström 1980, Hellspong, Löfgren, 1972
9 ETS p 57, Liljeström 1979
10 Holgersson 1977
11 ETS p 55, de Mause, 1974
12 ETS pp 58–59, Ambjörnsson, 1978
13 ETS pp 276–280, Holter, 1976, Frykman, Löfgren 1979
14 ETS pp 369–373
15 ETS p 371, Folmer 1980
16 ETS pp 190–192, Frykman, Löfgren, 1979
17 Olsson 1980
18 ETS pp 277–280, Frykman, Löfgren, 1979
19 ETS pp 231–232
20 ETS pp 409–415, Lundkvist 1977
21 ETS pp 417–419
22 ETS pp 420–422, Jansson 1977
23 ETS pp 415–417
24 Henschen *et al* 1979
25 Henschen *et al* 1979
26 Kieselberg 1979

Chapter 2

1 ETS pp 267–270, Donzelot 1979
2 Donzelot 1979
3 ETS p 270
4 ETS p 268, Donzelot 1979
5 Foucault 1978

6 Donzelot 1979
7 ETS p 308
8 Seabrook, 1979
9 ETS pp 63–65
10 ETS p 66. Lohmann 1972
11 Beckman, 1980
12 ETS pp 69–71, 313–315, Lasch 1978, Ronnby 1977, Hellberg 1978 NAVF, 1977, Johansson–Hedberg 1979

Chapter 3

1 Kieselberg 1979
2 ETS p 61, Gillis, 1974
3 ETS pp 384–386
4 ETS p 47, 71. Schedin 1977
5 Göransson 1980
6 Gillis 1974
7 ETS pp 427–428, Liljeström 1980
8 Dale, 1981
9 ETS p 427
10 Göransson 1980
11 ETS pp 104–105, Dahlgren 1981
12 ETS p 65
13 Dale 1981
14 ETS pp 65–66, Än sén då?, Statens ungdomsråd 1980
15 ETS pp 73–81, Lasch 1978
16 Lasch 1978
17 ETS p 178, Ziehe, 1978
18 Nordland 1981
19 ETS pp 72–73

Chapter 4

1 ETS pp 41–47, Liljeström *et al* 1981
2 ETS p 342, Edin, Hedborg 1980
3 ETS pp 47–48
4 ETS pp 99–102, Dahlgren 1981
5 ETS pp 101–102
6 ETS pp 343–347, Gorz 1979, Hirsch 1977

*ETS = Ej till salu, the original full-length report, available only in Swedish.

195

7   Gorz 1979
8   ETS pp 347–348
9   ETS pp 349–353. Braverman 1974
10 ETS pp 353–355, Ottomeyer 1978.
    Gardell 1976
11 Ottomeyer 1978
12 Lasch 1977
13 MacIntyre 1981
14 ETS pp 189–190, Liljeström 1979
15 ETS pp 188–189
16 Statens ungdomsråd 1978
17 Statens ungdomsråd 1978
18 Sellerberg 1976
19 Jundin 1979
20 Ward 1977
21 Statens ungdomsråd 1980
22 ETS p 104, Kälvesten, Ödman 1979
23 Bjurström 1980
24 ETS pp 223–226, Hall et al 1976
25 ETS pp 188–189
26 ETS pp 194–203
27 ETS pp 222–223, Mitchell 1979,
    Ziehe 1978, Lasch 1978
28 Statens ungdomsråd 1978, Zetterberg
    1979
29 ETS pp 193–194
30 ETS pp 194–203, Statens ungdoms-
    råd, 1979, 1980
31 ETS pp 193–203
32 ETS pp 205–215, Belert 1979,
    Bettelheim 1975
33 ETS p 212
34 Bettelheim 1975
35 ETS pp 207–213. Fausing 1980
36 ETS pp 207–213, Holm 1979
37 ETS pp 121–146, Jonsson 1979
38 ETS pp 138–145, Statens ungdoms-
    råd 1978, 1979
39 Packard 1957
40 ETS p 128, Key 1976
41 ETS pp 129–134, Friberg, Körne-
    mark 1979
42 ETS pp 146–185
43 Williamson 1978
44 ETS pp 223–228, Statens ungdoms-
    råd 1980
45 Hall et al 1976
46 Clarke, Jefferson 1976

Chapter 5

1   ETS p 451, Liljeström et al 1981,
    Kosik 1978
2   ETS p 445
3   ETS pp 456–458

4   Ingelstam 1980
5   ETS p 456, 460
6   ETS pp 450–451, Berger, Luckman
    1966
7   ETS p 448
8   ETS p 595
9   ETS pp 448–450, Liljeström 1981
10 Liljeström 1981
11 ETS p 450, Allardt 1975, Fromm
    1976
12 ETS p 453
13 ETS p 453
14 ETS p 457, 462–464
15 ETS pp 591–592
16 ETS pp 470–471
17 ETS p 460
18 ETS pp 592–595
19 ETS p 476
20 ETS pp 477–480
21 ETS p 481
22 ETS pp 485–488
23 ETS pp 492–493
24 ETS pp 488–490
25 ETS p 484
26 ETS pp 484–485
27 ETS pp 499–500
28 ETS pp 606–641, Nilsson Wadeskog
    1981
29 ETS pp 504–505
30 ETS pp 506–508, Beckman 1981
31 ETS pp 508–509
32 ETS p 510
33 ETS pp 606–641
34 ETS pp 500–503
35 ETS pp 521–522
36 ETS p 522
37 ETS pp 526–530
38 ETS pp 530–531
39 ETS pp 531–532
40 ETS p 538
41 ETS pp 532–533
42 ETS pp 533–535
43 ETS p 563
44 ETS pp 564–565
45 ETS p 571
46 For example, the associations' colla-
    boration in schools.
47 ETS p 566
48 ETS p 575
49 ETS pp 578–579
50 ETS pp 461–462
51 ETS p 462
52 ETS p 464
53 Olsson 1980
54 ETS pp 600–602
55 ETS pp 493–498, Henriksson 1980

Bibliography

Ambjörnsson, R, Familjeporträtt (Family Portraits); Gidlunds, 1978

Allardt, E, Att ha, att älska, att vara—om välfärd i Norden (To have, to love, to be—welfare in Scandinavia); Argos, 1975

Beckman, S, Kärlek på tjänstetid (Love in working hours); Arbetslivscentrum, Stockholm, 1981

Belert, K, Fantasi och samfund (Fantasy and society); Bixen: 1979, 3

Berger, L and Luckman, T, The Social Construction of Reality—A Treatise in the Sociology of Knowledge; 1966

Bettelheim, B, The Uses of Enchantment. The Meaning and Importance of Fairy Tales; 1975

Bjurström E, Generationsupproret (The generation uprising); Wahlström & Widstrand, 1980

Braverman, H, Labour and Monopoly Capital—The Degradation of Work in the Twentieth Century; Monthly Review Press, 1974

Clarke, J and Jefferson, T, Working Class Youth Culture (in Mungham, G and Pearson, G, Working Class Youth Culture; Routledge and Kegan Paul, London, 1976)

Dale, E L, Vad är uppfostran? (What is upbringing?); Natur och Kultur, 1981

Dahlström, E and Liljeström, R, Det patriarkala arvet (The patriarchal heritage); Sociologisk forskning no 2, 1981

DeMause, L, The History of Childhood; Psychohistory Press, New York, 1974

Donzelot, J, The Policing of Families; Pantheon Books, New York, 1979

Edin, P-O and Hedborg, A, Det nya uppdraget (The new task); Tiden, 1980

Fausing, B, Almagt og Afmagt—om oplevelsemønstre af perceptionsformer (Omnipotence and impotence—experience patterns of forms of perception)—paper to International Mass-media Seminar, Summer, 1980

Folmer, A, Fritidens historia (The history of leisure); På fritid: 1980, 3

Foucault, M, The History of Sexuality; Random House, 1978

Friberg, G and Körnemark, L, Reklam till barn (Advertising to children); Stencil, 1979

Fromm, E, Att ha eller att vara (To have or to be); Natur och Kultur, 1976

Frykman, J and Löfgren, O, Den kultiverade människan (The cultivated human being); Liber Läromedel, 1979

Gardell, B, Arbetsinnehåll och Livskvalitet (Work content and quality of life); Prisma, 1976

Gillis, J R, Youth History; Academic Press, New York, 1974

Gorz, A, Ekologi och politik (Ecology and politics); Bokomotiv, 1979

Göransson, E, Stockholmsungdomarnas fritidsvanor—en delstudie av ungdomarnas deltagande i föreningslivet (The leisure habits of Stockholm youth—part of a study of the participation of youth in associations); Stockholms kommun, 1980; (Part 12 of the report 'Unsuitable Youth Environments')

Hall, S, *et al.,* Resistance Through Rituals; Hutchinson, London, 1976

Hanssen, B, Familj, hushåll, släkt (Family, household, relatives); Gidlunds, 1978

Hellberg, I, Studier i professionell organisation (Studies in professional organisation); Sociologiska institutionen, Göteborgs universitet, 1978

Hellspong, M and Löfgren, O, Land och stad (Country and town); Gleerup, 1972

Henriksson, B, Samhället utanför skolan (The community outside school), in Naeslund, J (ed); Begrepp, motiv, termer—en handbok till arbetet med LGR 80 (Concepts, motives, terms—a handbook for work with LGR 80); Liber/ Utbildningsförlaget, 1980

Henschen, H (ed) *et al.,* Barn i stan (Children in the city); Folksam/Stockholms Stadsmuseum, Tiden, 1979

Hirsch, F, The Social Limits to Growth; Routledge & Kegan Paul, Cambridge, Mass., 1977

Holgersson, L, Socialvården: en fråga om människosyn (Social care: a question of human attitudes); Tiden, 1977

Holm, B, Kampen om fantasiproduktionen (The struggle over fantasy production); Ord och Bild: 1976, 6

Holm, B, Sanningen om Sherlock Holmes (The truth about Sherlock Holmes); Krut: 1979, 9

Holter, H, *et al.,* Familjen I klassamhället (The family in class society); Bonniers, 1976

Ingelstam, L, Arbetets värde och tidens bruk (The value of work and the use of time); LiberFörlag/Sekretariatet för framtidsstudier, 1980

Jansson, L, Socialdemokratiska ungdomsklubben AKTIV 1923–1933: en jämförande studie av arbetarrörelsens kulturmiljö (The Social Democratic youth club AKTIV, 1923–1933, a comparative study of the cultural environment of the labour movement); Institutet för folklivsforskning, Stockholms universitet, 1977

Johansson-Hedberg, B, Barn-Sverige (Children-Sweden); LiberFörlag/Sekretariatet för framtidsstudier, 1979

Jonsson, E, Konsten att förföra konsumenten—en kritisk granskning av läroböcker i marknadsföring (The art of seducing the consumer—a critical appraisal of textbooks in marketing); Rabén & Sjögren, 1979 (TemaNova)

Jundin, S, När barn köper (When children buy things); Ekonomiska forskningsinstitutet vid Handelshögskolan i Stockholm, 1979

Key, W-B, Media sexploitation; Prentice Hall, Eaglewood Cliffs, NJ., 1976

Kieselberg, S, Maendenes historie—en moral-sociologisk studie i den traditionelle manderolle (The history of men—a moral-sociological study of the traditional man's role); Rhodos, Copenhagen, 1979

Kosik, K, Det konkretas dialektik (The dialectics of the concrete); Röda bokförlaget, 1978

Kälvesten, A-L and Ödman, M, Barn i 5 länder tecknar och tänker (Children in 5 countries—their drawings and thoughts); Liber/Utbildningsförlaget, 1979

198

Lasch, C, Culture of Narcissism; Norton, New York, 1978

Lasch, C, Haven in a Heartless World; Basic Books, New York, 1977

Le Roy Ladurie, E, Montaillou—village occitan de 1294 à 1324; Gallimard, 1975

Liljeström, R, Kultur och arbete (Culture and work); LiberFörlag/Sekretariatet för framtidsstudier, 1979

Liljeström, R, Barn och kultur (Children and culture); Stencil, 1980

Liljeström, R, Livskvalitet i baradoms-och ungdomsår (The quality of life in childhood and adolescence); in Normgruppen: Normer och normlöshet (Norms and normlessness); Liber, 1980

Liljeström, R, et al., Arbetarkvinnor (Working Class Women); Tiden, 1981

Lohmann, H, Psykisk hälsa och mänsklig miljö (Mental health and human environment); Socialstyrelsen/Allmänna Förlaget, 1972, (Socialstyrelsen redovisar: 30)

Lundkvist, S, Folkrörelserna i det svenska samhället 1850−1920 (The popular movements in Swedish society, 1850−1920); Sober, 1977

MacIntyre, A, After Virtue—A Study in Moral Theory; University of Notre Dame Press, 1981

Mitchell, R, Youth Socialisation and Cultural Industries; paper for UNESCO: Stencil, 1979

Norland, E, Ungdom i Norge (Youth in Norway); Universitetsförlaget, Oslo, 1979

Nordland, E, Ungdomens konsumtionsmönster och marknadsekonomin (Young people's patterns of consumption and the market economy); Stencil, 1979

Nordland, E, 'Krig ger "mening" åt de ungas liv' ('War gives a "purpose" to youngsters' lives'); article in Svenska Dagbladet, 23.06.81

Norges Almenvitenskapelige Forskningsråd (NAVF) (Norwegian Scientific Research Council), Profesjonaliseringsamfunnsbehov eller gruppintresse? (Needs of professionalised society or group interests?); Utredningsinstitutt, 1977:7

Olsson, J, Förorten, grannskapsarbete och förändringsmöjligheter (The suburb, neighbourhood work and opportunities for change); Delegationen för social forskning, Rapport 1979:1

Olsson, L, När barn var lönsamma (When children were profitable); Tiden, 1980

Ottomeyer, K, Ökonomische Zwänge und Menschliche Beziehungen; Rowohlt, 1977.

Packard, V, The Hidden Persuaders; McKay, New York, 1957

Ronnby, A, Socialpolitisk kritik (Sociopolitical criticism); Student-litteratur, 1977

Schedin, G, Ungdomsutveckling och psykologi (Youth development and psychology); Natur och kultur, 1977

Seabrook, J, What Went Wrong?; Pantheon, New York, 1979

Sellerberg, A-M, En sociologisk analys av konsumtionsvanor (A sociological analysis of consumer habits); Sociologiska institutionen, Lunds universitet, 1976

Statens Ungdomsråd, (Swedish National Youth Council), At any price; 1978

Statens Ungdomsråd, Rullbrädesmarknaden (The skateboard market); LiberFörlag, 1978 (Report series Till varje pris (At any price)—1)

Statens Ungdomsråd, Skateboardåkaren (The skateboard rider)/B Schelin; LiberFörlag, 1979 (Report series Till varje pris—2)

Statens Ungdomsråd, I nattens ljus. Dans i Sverige (In the light of the night. Dancing in Sweden), 1979/L Silfverhjelm, P Strandberg; Liber Förlag, 1979 (Report series Till Varje pris—3)

Statens Ungdomsråd, Kila på bio. Köp en livsstil (Rush to the cinema. Buy a life-style)/O Breitenstein, E Wikander; Liber Förlag, 1979 (Report series Till varje pris—4)

Statens Ungdomsråd, Musik på löpande band (Music on a production line)/ E Bjurström; Liber Förlag, 1980 (Report series Till varje pris—5)

Statens Ungdomsråd, Trots allt. Alternativen lever (In spite of everything. The alternatives live on.)/I Ärlemalm; Liber Förlag, 1980 (Report series Till varje pris—6)

Statens Ungdomsråd, Smockor och smek. Hotande läsning—om ungdomstidningar (Cuffs and caresses. Menacing reading—about youth magazines)/I Jakalas; Liber Förlag, 1980 (Report series Till varje pris—7)

Statens Ungdomsråd, Än sen då? Röster om framtid (What then? Voices on the future); Liber Förlag, 1980 (Report series Till varje pris—8)

Statens Ungdomsråd, Ungdomars konsumtion (Youth consumption)/R Persson, A Dahlgren, 1981

Statens Ungdomsråd, Att vara 11 år och att vara 16 (Being 11 years old and being 16)/A Dahlgren, 1981

Statens Ungdomsråd, Det blir för dyrt (It will cost too much)/I Nilsson, A Wadeskog, 1981

Ward, S, *inter alia*, How children learn to buy; Sage Publications, California, 1977

Williamson, J, Decoding advertisements—ideology and meaning in advertising; Marion Boyars, London, 1978

Zetterberg, H, Värderingar i ungdomsvärlden. De snabba förändringarnas karusell (Values in the youth world. The carousel of swift changes) in Statens ungdomsråd: Ungdomen, föreningslivet och kommersialism (Youth, associations and commercialism); 1979

Ziehe, T, Pubertät und Narzissmus; Europäische Verlagsanstalt, Frankfurt, 1978

Bibliography to Appendix 3 *a few facts*

1 Statistisk årsbok 1980/Statistiska centralbyrån (Statistical
   Yearbook 1980/Central Bureau for Statistics); Liber Förlag;
   Stockholm, 1980.

2 Törnquist, K: Ungdom och Säkerketspolitik (Youth and Policy on
   Security) Beredskapsnämnden för psykologiskt försvar (Council for
   psychological defence); Stockholm, 1979.

3 Klackenberg-Larsson, J; Björkman, K: Storstadsungdomarnas syn
   på tillvaron (City youth's view of existence); Socialmedicinsk
   tidskrift (Socio-medical Journal) 1980:2.

4 Statens ungdomsråd (Swedish National Youth Council):
   Ungdomens fritid och samhällssyn (Youth leisure and view of
   society)/R Persson, A Dahlgren; Prisma, 1975.

5 Kälvesten, A-L; Ödman, M; Barn i 5 länder tecknar och tänker
   (Children in 5 countries, their drawings and thoughts);
   Liber/Utbildningsförlaget, Stockholm, 1979.

6 See 3

7 Skolöverstyrelsen (SÖ): Tonåringarna och livet (Teenagers and
   life); 1980.

8 See 7

9 See 3

10 See 4

11 Statens Ungdomsråd (Swedish National Youth Council):
   Ungdomarnas konsumtion (Youth consumption)/R Persson, A
   Dahlgren; 1978.

12-15 see 11

16 Jundin, S: När barn köper (When children make purchases);
   Institute for Economic Research, Handelshögskolan, Stockholm,
   1979.

17 See 11

18-21 See 16

22 Sellerberg, A-M: En sociologisk analys av konsumtionsvanor (A
   sociological analysis of consumer habits); Department of
   Sociology, Lund University, 1976.

23-27 See 22

28 Konsumentverket (Consumer Commission): Konsument 79
   (Consumer 79), 1980.

29, 30 See 16

31-33 See 28

34 Nordiska ministerrådet (Nordic Council of Ministers): Reklam i
   skolan (Advertising in schools); Stockholm, 1971 (NU-series B:
   1979:1).

35 Nilsson, C: Hemma i mediasamhället (At home in the mass-media
   society); Stockholm, 1978 (SR/PUB 1978:11).

36-38 See 35

39 Statens ungdomsråd (Swedish National Youth Council): Att vara
    11 år och att vara 16 (Being 11 years old and being 16)/A
    Dahlgren, 1981.
40–70 See 39
71 Statiska Centralbyrån (SCB) (Central Bureau for Statistics):
    Statistiska meddelanden (Statistical communications) U 1980:17.
72 See 71
73, 74 See 3
75 Andersson, B; et al: Segregation och särbehandling i grundskolan
    (Segregation and special treatment in comprehensive schools)
    Sociology Department, Lund University, 1977.
76 See 75
77 SCB: Statistiska meddelanden (Statistical communications); U
    1980:13.
78 SCB: Statistiska meddelanden U 1980:16.
79 See 78
80, 81 See 1
82 Sundström, G: Omsorg oss emellan (Caring, between ourselves);
    Liber Förlag-Secretariat for Future Studies, Stockholm, 1980.
83 See 82
84 See 1
85 SCB: Ung 79 (Young 79); (PM 1979:6).
86–88 See 82
89 Johansson, S: Barnens välfärd (Children's welfare); Stencil, 1980.
90 Socialstyrelsen (Social Welfare Authority): Barnomsorg i siffror
    1979–83 (Child-care in Statistics 1979–83); Barnomsorgsplanering
    (Child-care planning), 1979:2.
91 Filipsson, L; Schyller, J: Barns tittande i maj 1979 (Children's
    viewing in May 1979); Stockholm, 1980. (SR/PUB: 1980:2).
92, 93 See 91
94 See 3
95, 96 See 7
97 See 4
98–103 See 3
104 See 4
105 See 3
106, 107 See 1
108 Gaunt, L: 205 skolbarns bostadsanvändning (205 schoolchildren's
    use of the home); Statens institut för byggnadsforskning (National
    institute for building research); Bulletin M79:7; Gävle, 1979.
109 Socialstyrelsen: Alkoholbyrån (The alcohol bureau); PM
    1980–09–19.
110 Brottsförebyggande rådet (BRÅ) (Council for crime prevention):
    Ungdomsbrottslighet (Youth crime); Stockholm, 1980.
    BRÅ-S:1980:1.
111, 112 See 110

113 See 89
114 Institutet för marknadsundersökningar (Institute for market research) IMU: Langing—en undersökning genomförd för socialdepartementet jan–feb 1980 (Selling alcohol to underage drinkers—an investigation carried out for the Department of Social Welfare, Jan–Feb 1980.)
115–122 See 114
123 Skolöverstyrelsen (SÖ): Tonåringarna och drogerna (Teenagers and drugs), 1980.
124–126 See 123
127 Arbetsmarknadsstyrelse (AMS) (Labour Market Commission): Yrkesväglednings-enheten (The career counselling unit) PM 1981–02–17.
128 See 127
129 Skolöverstyrelse (SÖ): Utbildning och arbetsförhållanden bland 16–19 åringar (Education and working conditions among 16–19 year olds) (Report 1978–12–15)
130 Invandrarverket (Immigration Authority): Invandrarungdomarna (Immigrant Youth); 1981.
131 Filipson, L: Skolbarn och etermedia (Schoolchildren and the media); Stockholm, 1980 (SR/PUB: 1980:20).
132 Göransson, E; Nyman, B: Stockholmsungdomarna inför 80-talet (Stockholm youth, entering the 80s); Stockholms kommun, 1980 (Part 10 of report 'Olämpliga ungdomsmiljöer' ('Unsuitable youth environments').
133 Nyström: Förströelse eller förstörelse (Amusement or destruction) 'Vi' No 17/1979.
134 See 133
135 See 39
136 See 131
137 Schyller, J; Filipson, L: 1000 och en siffra om barns läggvanor—biovanor—TV-tittarsituation—rädsla vid TV-program—sagoläsning (1,000 and one figures on children's habits —going to bed—cinema—TV-viewing—fear of TV-programmes— reading stories); Stockholm, 1979. (SR/PUB: 1979:16.)
138–140 See 131
141 Statens Kulturråd/SCB (Swedish National Culture Council): Kulturstatistik (Culture Statistics); Liber Förlag: Stockholm, 1981.
142 Statens Ungdomsråd: Kila på bio. Köp en livsstil (Rush to the cinema. Buy a lifestyle)/O Breitenstein, E Wikander; LiberFörlag; Stockholm, 1979. Report Series *Till Varje Pris*, 4 (At Any Price, 4).
143 Statens Ungdomsråd: Smockor och smek. Hotande läsning—om ungdomstidningarna (Smacks and caresses—menacing reading—on youth magazines)/I Jakalas; Liber Förlag; Stockholm, 1980. (Report Series *Till varje pris*, 7 (At Any Price, 7).

144   See 141
145   Statens Ungdomsråd: Massor i rörelse. Föreningarna i Sverige (The masses on the move. Associations in Sweden); Liber Förlag, Stockholm, 1980.
146   See 145
147   See 4
148   Göransson, E: Stockholmsungdomarnas fritidsvanor—en delstudie av ungdomarnas deltagande i föreningslivet (Leisure habits of Stockholm youth—a part study of youth participation in association activities): Stockholms kommun, 1980. (Part 12 of the Report 'Unsuitable Youth Environments').
149   See 4
150   Statens Ungdomsråd: Försöksverksamheten i Gävle 1975-77. Skolungdomarnas syn på föreningar, enkät, 1977. (Research in Gävle 1975-77. The views of school pupils on associations, questionnaire, 1977): Stockholm, 1977. (Projektrapport: 21).
151   SIFO: Bakgrundsrapport: ungdomsundersökningen vintern 1979/80 (Background report: Youth survey/Winter 1979/80).
152   Malmö fritidsförvaltning (Malmö leisure authority): Skolbarn i föreningar 1977 (Schoolchildren in associations 1977) (Report 1980:1).
153   See 145
154-158 See 4
159-172 See 145
173-182 See 39